1

Al-Qaeda and Its Fearsome Tentacles

America has now reasons to feel happy with President Musharraf's fight against Al-Qaeda terrorism. On July 13, Pakistani authorities arrested Mohammed Naeem Noor Khan at Lahore Airport. Khan is an engineer and had been using Islamic websites to transmit encrypted instructions to Al-Qaeda cells. Khan was assisting in evaluation of potential targets and served as a clearinghouse of information. Khan used different internet cafes and relayed coded messages through secure websites that required a number of passwords to gain entry. After the arrest under the supervision of Pakistani officers, Khan sent e-mails to other Al-Qaeda members who were unaware that he has been arrested thus allowing the investigators to pinpoint the coordinates of the key operatives. The information gathered from Khan led to the arrest of other important Al-Qaeda operatives including some top leaders.

On July 25, 2004, a top Al-Qaeda leader, Tanzanian born Ahmad Khalfan Ghailani who had $ 5 million on his head was captured in Gujarat 160 km south of Islamabad. Ghailani was wanted by the United States for his role in 1998 bombings of American Embassies in East Africa that

killed 224 people. Ghailani was captured with 13 others after a 14-hour gun battle with the security forces. This raid uncovered 3 laptop computers and 51 data-rich disks. In the computers were stored 500 photographs of potential targets in U.S.A., detailed analysis of their vulnerabilities and also communications among some of the wanted terrorists of the world. Information elicited was very detailed and specific. A senior U.S. intelligence officer called them "*unprecedented treasure trove of information*". Ghailani who is in his early thirties is the senior most Al-Qaeda operative caught in Pakistan since the arrest in March, 2003 of Khalid Sheikh Mohammad, the mastermind of 9/11 attacks on New York and Washington.

Though most of the data contained in the hard drives were at least three years old, the intelligence analysts point out that the Al-Qaeda has cased targets for years before attacking. Preparations of 1998 bombing of the two U.S. embassies began in 1993. Though the surveillance for information in the hard-disc was done mostly in 2000, information was also periodically updated. The discs detailed the operatives' extensive reconnaissance of buildings like New York's Stock Exchange, Citi Group Building, Washington HQ of both IMF and World Bank. The surveillance reports note the structure of the buildings, their security arrangements, the flow of traffic outside the buildings and whether explosives could melt steel underpinnings of a building etc. All this prompted the security alert in New York and Washington. The Home Land Security Chief Tom Ridge went public with the names of the targeted buildings arguing that employees of the

targeted companies could be helpful in reporting anything relevant or in unravelling the mystery of those who had done the surveillance.

The information provided by Khan and his files led to arrest of another 13 suspected terrorists in Britain on August 3rd 2004. Among them was one Abu-Isa-Al-Hindi who was sent to the U.S.A. by Osama-Bin-Laden in 2001 to case targets. He is also wanted for plotting attack on Heathrow Airport that took place last year. Al-Hindi has been identified by British Intelligence Services as a young Hindu convert who had published under 'nom-de-guerre' a memoir of his *jihad* in Kashmir.

The Pakistan Government suspended more than 60 local policemen including several officers for negligence in detecting and monitoring the foreigners who could be captured only with American assistance. In the wake of the arrest of Al-Qaeda operatives came an attack on Shaukat Aziz, the present Prime Minister of Pakistan, in which nine people including his driver were killed. A group calling itself '*Islambouli Brigades*' of Al-Qaeda claimed responsibility and declared that it would target pro-American Government leaders in Pakistan. The outfit is named after the leader of militant Islamic group, which assassinated Egyptian President, Anwar Sadat in 1981. This is for the first time Al-Qaeda has claimed responsibility for terrorist attacks in Pakistan and is unlikely to be the last.

Computer records, e-mail addresses and documents seized after the arrest of Md. Noor Khan show that new operatives are filling up Al-Qaeda ranks. The new evidence

suggest that Al-Qaeda has retained some elements of its previous centralized command and communication structure using computer experts like Khan to relay messages and directions from leaders to subordinates in countries like Britain, Turkey and Nigeria.

It now seems that Al-Qaeda and the Taliban uprooted from Afghanistan are using Pakistan, their former transit station, as a temporary staging ground for terrorist operations. Some of them created network within Pakistan taking advantage of poor law enforcement and the state's sympathetic attitude towards pan-Islamic militancy.

Musharraf remains one of the prime targets of Al-Qaeda. Last year Ayman-Al-Zawahari, the Egyptian Second-in-Command of Osama-Bin-Laden, instructed the faithful to kill him and since then Islamic activists have launched two near-fatal attacks on the President. Other important pro-American politicians of Pakistan are also in Al-Qaeda's hit list. Musharraf has now admitted before foreign correspondents (*Time*, August 23, 2004) that in March 2004, a terrorist summit was held in the tribal province of Waziristan. Al-Qaeda terrorists from all-over the world slipped into Pakistan to attend it and work out strategies for attacking U.S.A. Some of the terrorists who participated in the summit like Abu-Isa-Al-Hindi, Muhammad Junaid Babar have been arrested. But others are still at large. One of them is a dreaded el-Shukrizumah 29, an Arab Guyanese bomb maker and a commercial pilot. FBI agents call el-Shukrizumah, the next Atta after Mohammed Atta, the Egyptian ring leader of the 9/11 attacks.

Indeed, U.S.A.'s success in apprehension of the well-known and infamous terrorists has been limited. In October, 2001, America produced a list of 22 most wanted terrorists offering rewards up to $ 5 million for information leading to their arrests. So far only a few of this list of twenty-two have been captured or killed, namely, Muhammad Atef, Khalid Sheikh Mohammad and Ahmed Khalfan Ghailani. The rest remains at large.

As Presidential election campaign in America gains momentum, the Bush administration will rely heavily on Pakistan's President to capture top Al-Qaeda men. During their recent visits Deputy Secretary, State Department, Richard Armitage and General Abizaid have pressed on Musharraf to capture High Value Targets (HVT) as early as possible. It remains to be seen if Musharraf is able to do this before the American election. The string of arrests in Pakistan may have disrupted a plot but may not have derailed it. Further though Pakistan is helping America to nab Al-Qaeda terrorists, Musharraf has always provided support to local Islamic groups who provide succour to Al-Qaeda. This policy of supporting the local militants while banning others does not work in practice. Kashmiri Jehadis and Kandahari Jehadis forge links. The group called Herkat-ul-Jihad-I-Islami, which keeps close links with Al-Qaeda after being banned two years ago has re-emerged under different names.

Earlier interrogation of Khalid Sheikh Mohammad, an alleged mastermind of September 11 attacks, who was arrested in Rawalpindi in March, 2003, revealed that Al-Qaeda has not been dispersed totally by American attacks

on Afghanistan. Even after receiving hard knocks, its organizational core perhaps remains intact. Experts estimate that Al-Qaeda is no longer a omnipotent hydra of destruction and its capacity for launching elaborately planned spectacular attacks has diminished, but more small-scale and randomly directed attacks, such as this year's bombings in Madrid, will be carried out by individuals who have only a passing contact with the Al-Qaeda organisation. Thus, through massive attacks like that of 9/11 by Al-Qaeda are very unlikely, though not impossible, decentralized terrorists will continue to haunt U.S.A. and its allies. Even if Bin-Laden is knocked out, the battle will not be over.

The U.S. National Commission investigating September 11, 2001, terrorist attacks has correctly pointed out that Al-Qaeda now represents an "ideological movement and not a finite group of people. In this way, it has transformed itself to a decentralized force". Bin-Laden may be limited in his ability to organise major attacks from his hideouts but his message of inspiration to a new generation of terrorists, particularly in the embittered Muslim world, would influence many. In its second coming as the standard bearer of extremist ideology, Al-Qaeda is scoring a nightmarish success and inspiring generations of embittered Muslim youth. This rampant dissemination of Al-Qaeda's ideology has made it easier for the group to recruit individuals.

In the past three years, the U.S.A. has put the fight against terrorism at the top of its global agenda. It has added about $ 200 billion to its spending on international

affairs and homeland security. But U.S.A. has to get global cooperation in fighting this long struggle. Without a wide multi-lateral system to fight against this common scourge, there will be too many loopholes for the terrorists to exploit.

2

Resurgence of Al-Qaeda: Testing Time for Musharraf

In his annual threat assessment on January 11, 2007, John Negroponte, America's outgoing intelligence chief, spoke about the worrying signs of Al-Qaeda's revival. According to him Al-Qaeda was not on the run but on the march. Its "*core*" leadership was resilient. Its hiding places in Pakistan were "*secure*" and it was cultivating stronger operational connections and relationships with affiliated groups in the Middle-East, North Africa and Europe. Earlier in November Eliza Manninghan Buller, head of MI5 of British Intelligence, also spoke about Al-Queda's growing and extensive scale of operations. Negroponte called Pakistan an important ally but also a "*major source of Islamic extremism*".

According to a *New York Times* report Al-Qaeda leaderships working from the bases of North Waziristan have successfully revived the terrorist network. Pakistan Government discounted these allegations as absurd and took the stand that with the presence of nearly 80,000 Pakistani troops in tribal regions it was not possible for Al-Qaeda to establish bases in the region. However,

Afghanistan and American officials have not accepted Pakistan's viewpoint and laid blame on it for providing havens for the Talibans. General Eikenbery, Senior Army Commander in Afghanistan, has also pointed out that the deal which Pakistan Government struck on peace agreement with the tribal leaders during last September has not helped matters and only enabled the militants to strengthen and regroup themselves. The Governor of North East Frontier Province brokered the deal.

During his visit to Washington, Pakistan President Musharraf obtained President Bush's endorsement for it, but things have not improved after the deal and the militants continue their depredations. They have also replaced the tribal leaders who earlier used to mediate with the Central administration and are running virtually a parallel administration. In the month of November 2006, an air strike levelled a *madrasa* in North-Western Province killing 80 people. Though the Pakistan administration owned the responsibility, many people blamed an American drone for the attack. There was violent response; a suicide bomb attack killed about 40 army recruits at Dargan. Violence now has become endemic not only in the tribal areas but also in the settled areas of North-Western Province dominated by ethnic Pashtoons. Earlier, the Afghanistan Government had also produced the video of a captured Taliban spokesman making the startling allegation that the Taliban leader Mulla Omar was under Pakistan's protection in the city of Quetta. Pakistan of course pooh-poohed the claim. In its turn Pakistan has proposed the idea of fencing and mining 2500 km border

with Afghanistan ostensibly to restrict the movement of the Taliban fighters. Afghanistan as well as UN objected to it because it would endanger civilian lives and also divide Pakistan tribes straddling the frontier.

According to U.S. officials there is increasing evidence that Osama-Bin-Ladan and his deputy Ayman-Al-Jawahari are steadily building an operational hub in the mountainous tribal areas of North Waziristan. The view held by Bush administration till recently was that Osama-Bin-Laden and Al-Jawahari were detached from their supporters and not in control of Al-Qaeda. The view is now changing. U.S.A. through spy satellites has identified many Al-Qaeda compounds in North Waziristan and these compounds operate under loose command structure and run by militants affiliated to Al-Qaeda. They receive guidance from their commanders and also from Al-Jawahari. These terrorist networks, despite more than 5 years of campaign to dismantle them, according to Intelligence agencies are gaining strength.

The present Director of National Intelligence Admiral Mike McConnell has deposed before the Senate Arms Committee that Al-Qaeda leadership has established itself in the region and is running the training camps. According to him with the signing of agreement with the tribal areas in the frontier areas, the capabilities of Al-Qaeda have increased. He also expressed the grim fear that next Al-Qaeda attack on U.S. would be planned and come out of the Al-Qaeda leadership based in Pakistan.

The resurgence of Al-Qaeda has ignited the debate in the corridors of power in Washington as how to address

AF654385

Contents

Acknowledgements

I owe a deep debt of gratitude to some of my friends in Indian Police Service and academics in the Institute of Social Sciences for their suggestions and insightful observations. They have enlightened me from time to time with their analytical views and comments. I am sincerely grateful to Shri Ravindra Kumar, Editor Statesman for giving permission to incorporate in the book some of the articles earlier published in the Statesman.

Sankar Sen

Further, Pakistan also continues to aid and abet the terrorist groups based in Pakistan to indulge in cross border terrorism. Some of these non-state actors have now turned against their masters and dragged Pakistan in the vortex of unending terrorist violence and disorder. The chickens have come home to roost. After the withdrawal of American troops in 2014, it is difficult to fathom the shape of things likely to emerge in Afghanistan and Pakistan's role in the unfolding scenario. With the new democratic regime under Nawaz Sharif it is hoped that Pakistan will not continue to muddy the waters in quest of strategic depth in Afghanistan. Indeed, Indian diplomacy and strategy will have to face a testing time.

I do hope that the bunch of articles will evoke interest among law enforcement officers, members of the armed forces, academics and public servants and will help in understanding the complexities of the situation emerging in our violent neighbourhood.

Preface

The book contains 18 articles which, appeared during last few years in different national dailies. They mainly deal with the turmoil and turbulence in Pakistan and Afghanistan and their likely fallouts. Developments in our violent neighbourhood have sinister implications for the country's security and safety. After the overthrow of the brutal Taliban regime by the US led international forces, it was hoped that Afghanistan will witness a new dawn. Unfortunately, that has not happened. Peace and stability continue to elude Afghanistan. With the covert support of Pakistan the remnants of the Taliban who are viscerally opposed to US backed Karzai government have unleashed waves of violence and disorder and resisted tooth and nail American presence in Afghanistan. Pakistan has dexterously played a double game and used the terrorists as proxies with the hope that a Taliban regime in Afghanistan after American withdrawal will subserve Pakistan's strategic interest and prevent India from exercising any influence in Afghanistan. Pakistan nurses an existential fear of encirclement by India.

© Sankar Sen

All rights reserved. No part of this work may be reproduced, stored, adapted, or transmitted in any form or by any means, electronic, mechanical, photocopying, micro-filming recording or otherwise, or translated in any language, without the prior written permission of the copyright owner and the publisher. The book is sold subject to the condition that it shall not, by way of trade or otherwise, be lent, resold, hired out, or otherwise circulated without prior publisher's written consent in any form of binding or cover other than that in which it is published.

The views and opinions expressed in this book are author(s) own and the facts reported by him/her have been verified to the extent possible, and the publishers are not in any way liable for the same.

ISBN-13 : 978-93-5125-010-4

First Published 2014

Published and Printed by

Concept
Since 1974

Concept Publishing Company Pvt. Ltd.
A/15-16, Commercial Block, Mohan Garden
New Delhi-110059 (India)
T: 25351460, 25351794, *F*: 091-11-25357109
E-mail: publishing@conceptpub.com, W: www.conceptpub.com
Editorial Office: H-13, Bali Nagar, New Delhi-110 015, India.

Cataloging in Publication Data--*Courtesy:* D.K. Agencies (P) Ltd. <docinfo@dkagencies.com>

Sen, Sankar, 1936-
Violent neighbourhood : turbulence in Pakistan and Afghanistan / Sankar Sen.
p. cm.
Articles; previously published.
Includes index.
ISBN 9789351250104

1. Afghanistan—Politics and government—2001-2. Afghanistan—Foreign relations—Pakistan. 3. Pakistan—Foreign relations—Afghanistan. 4. Terrorism Pakistan. 5. Terrorism—Afghanistan. 6. Violence—Pakistan. 7. Violence Afghanistan. I. Title.

DDC 320.95481 23

Violent Neighbourhood

Turbulence in Pakistan and Afghanistan

Sankar Sen, IPS

CONCEPT PUBLISHING COMPANY PVT. LTD.
NEW DELHI-110059

VIOLENT NEIGHBOURHOOD

About the Author

Sankar Sen (is presently Senior Fellow at the Institute of Social Sciences, New Delhi.) He is a distinguished Member of Indian Police Service from Odisha Cadre. He served in the Intelligence Bureau for seven years and also as the Additional Director General of the Border Security Force. He was the Director of the SVP National Police Academy (NPA), the Premier Police Institution for Training of IPS Officers in the country. As the Director of the NPA, he was responsible for many innovative changes in the training programmes of Indian Police Service Officers. On completion of his assignment at the NPA, he joined as the first Director General of the National Human Rights Commission (NHRC) and later on functioned as the Special Rapporteur in charge of custodial programmes of the NHRC. He was instrumental in building up an excellent investigation wing of the NHRC. He was awarded the Police Medal for Meritonous services and later police medal for Distinguished Service. A large number of his articles on law enforcement, terrorism, human rights and trafficking etc. have appeared in national dailies and well-known magazines in and outside the country. His books include *Indian Police Today, Police in Democratic Society, Human Rights in Developing Society, Terrorism and Drugs, Human Rights and Inhuman Wrongs, Trafficking in Women and Children, Enforcing Police Accountability through Civilian Oversight,* etc. Presently, he is working as the senior fellow and Head of Human Rights Wing in the Institute of Social Sciences

Pakistan's role as a sanctuary for the Talibans without undermining the Government of President Musharraf. It is learnt that Pentagon proposed to launch direct strikes on the alleged Al-Qaeda hideouts in Waziristan, but the State Department opposed it because it fears that such moves can destabilize Musharraf's Government and create more problems for America in the region. Increasingly, U.S.A. is gradually veering round to the view that Pakistan, through a critical ally, is failing to accomplish the task expected of it and it must take energetic steps to improve its capacity or allow U.S. and its allies to complete the task, which it is failing.

This view was echoed by the outgoing American Ambassador to Pakistan Ryan Crocker. Crocker told the American Foreign Relations Committee at the hearing on his nomination as U.S. Ambassador to Iraq that though Pakistan's commitment to counter terrorism remains high, its failure to contain the Talibans along its border with Afghanistan lies in its "*lack of capacity*".

Dick Cheney, the Vice President of America, in an unannounced visit to Pakistan, delivered an unusually tough message to Musharraf. He pressed Musharraf "*to do more*" to combat the Talibans' expected spring offensive against NATO in November. He warned him that Democratic Congress is likely to link further financial and military assistance to Pakistan to a certification by George Bush that General Musharraf is taking vigorous measures against both Al-Qaeda and Taliban in Pakistan's tribal borderlands. Pakistan has already received nearly $ 10 billion for supporting the war against terror since

September 2001 and is due to receive another $ 1 billion this year alone. Pakistan's Foreign Ministry has responded by declaring that Pakistan has done more than its share of the job and would not "*take dictation from anyone*". Musharraf has criticized Afghan President, Hamid Karzai for blaming Pakistan for his own government's lapses. Now, a senior U.S. Military Commander, Douglas Lute has disclosed that American and Afghan forces are engaged in hot pursuit of the terrorists across the border into Pakistan. This has created a ticklish situation for Musharraf.

Experts in the west such as Robert Kaplan and former officials such as Anthony C. Zimmi agree that Musharraf's importance lies not so much in his personal qualities but in the belief that whosoever comes after him would be a disaster. This may or may not be true. One of Pakistan's bargaining chips is the threat that it might become a rogue state if its friends did not help it. This suicide gambit, however, highlights vulnerability of Pakistan's moderate leadership and dangers from the Islamic radicals. Thus, for U.S.A., Pakistan is, as Stephen Cohen has perceptively said, in his "*Idea of Pakistan*", "*a part problem and a part solution*". An ally in the war against terrorism, it has also become a source of Islamic radicalism and nuclear proliferation. However, "devil you know" argument is a flawed one. Short-term policy built on support to a man without building up institutional capacities is based on a quicksand. Without meaningful democratization, political accountability and considerable economic development, the ruling establishment in Pakistan will find it increasingly difficult to neutralize the demands of the fundamentalists.

And it goes without saying that failure of Pakistan will be a multi-dimensional geo-strategic calamity, generating enormous uncertainties in the entire region. However, now there is hardening of the view in Pentagon that America should not fall for the Pakistan's practice whereby its rulers negotiate with a gun to their head. There is little risk of immediate collapse, and so USA must not be afraid to practice some tough love with Pakistan.

3

President Musharraf in a Cleft Stick

President Musharraf citing the need for unity of command has decided now to break the pledge of giving up the job of head of armed forces by the end of December 2004 and turn into a civilian leader. This was the promise he had earlier made to the opposition parties, and particularly to Muttahidda-Majlis-I-Amal (MMA), a coalition of Islamic parties for their support in Pakistan's Parliament. And now, not un-surprisingly he has refused to honour the promise. This is a big disappointment. It has become clear that Pakistan's fourth military saviour is totally dependent on his army position.

Opposition parties have begun protests and MMA have threatened to hold more demonstrations and derail the Parliament. Quazi Hussain Ahmad, Champion of Jamat-i-Islam, and to quote journalist Ayaz Amir, "Pakistan's foremost exponent of fake agitations" and another leader of religious parties, Fazlur Rahman has thundered that MMA will not accept General Musharraf as President, unless he takes off the uniform. However, MMA, despite brave posturings, will not push matter beyond a point of no return.

There is historic linkage between Pakistani army and these radical Islamic groups who have always received the support of ISI and army. Normally, military spymasters have fair measure of the verbal thunder of these fundamentalist groups. In October, 2002, election in Pakistan, MMA alliance polled nearly 11 per cent of the votes, which yielded sixty two seats. At the provincial level, it did its best in Pashtun dominated North-Western Frontier Province, where it won forty-seven per cent of the seats and formed the government. In Baluchistan MMA is a member of the Coalition Government. One of the important factors behind the unexpected electoral victory of MMA has been the support of Pakistan Government, and the difficulties it placed in the way of the mainstream parties. By assisting the MMA in the electoral campaign, Musharraf wanted to ensure that no opposition party won a clear majority in the election of 2002. But the clerics and religious parties are upset with Musharraf for his operations at American pressure against Al-Qaeda and the Taliban.

Musharraf expects that the prolongation of the army rule will not encounter serious opposition from the free world and there will be no pressure, particularly from America, on him to change his course. American backers of Musharraf feel that he is America's best bet and his importance lies not so much in his personal qualities but in the belief that whoever comes after him may be a disaster. This devil-you-know argument is, however flawed. Short-term policy based on support to a man without building up institutional capacities is based on quicksand. There always remains the danger that Musharraf like Ayub Khan and Zia-ul-Haq may slip into personalized rule and not know how and when to give up power. There is also a growing concern in Washington that a new spell of martial law will be counter-productive. If secular and provincial channels of expression are blocked, and if mainstream political parties are thwarted, this will only help the radical Islamists.

At the June, 2003, Camp David Summit, President Bush outlined three major goals of American policy towards Pakistan—keeping it as a partner in the war against terrorism, containing the spread of nuclear weapons and democratization. It will not be easy to persuade the present Pakistan Government that democratization is in Pakistan's own interest. Hostility of the army to the politicians cannot be erased overnight, but there should be pressure on Musharraf for army's staged withdrawal from politics. In Pakistan's national interest, restoration of a civil-military balance is necessary. America now wants Musharraf to change his political partners and build bridges with mainstream Pakistan People's Party (PPP) of Benazir Bhutto (now in exile). Benazir's husband Zardari, who had been languishing in prison for more than eight years, has been released. But Zardari was rearrested and his supporters beaten up when he had gone to Punjab; the stronghold of Pakistan Muslim League (PML), which is pro-Musharraf. Zardari then announced that he would carry on the campaign in the North Western Frontier Province and Baluchistan, which are controlled by MMA.

Proposed reconciliation with PPP puts Musharraf in a bind. If PPP were allowed to campaign freely, it would spell trouble for him as PPP is more popular than PML, which is backing him. If he turns against PPP, it will join hands with MMA and oppose his bid to continue as army chief. Already, Benazir Bhutto has urged opposition parties to step up pressure on Musharraf with a view to forcing him to shed the uniform. However, it is also a fact that PPP is engaged in behind-the-scene contact with ISI for striking a deal.

America's concern also stems from the fact that though Musharraf has launched operations against Al-Qaeda and hunted down foreign terrorists who threatened his own life, he has not vigorously pursued ex-Taliban leaders living inside the country. Islamabad's reluctance to crack down has enabled Afghan fundamentalists to use Pakistan as a haven to recruit fresh militants and launch counter-attacks against U.S. and Afghan forces. According to Afghan intelligence officials, Mullah Omar and other Taliban leaders are hiding in different areas of Pakistan. Recently, Omar issued a message renewing his call to fight the Americans. Allowing Taliban to remain free gives Pakistan a card to play if and when U.S. decides to leave Afghanistan. One of Pakistan's great bargaining chips is the threat that it might become a rogue state if its friends do not help it.

This '*suicide gambit*' however highlights the vulnerability of Pakistan's moderate leadership and dangers from Islamic radicals. For U.S.A., as Stephen Cohen puts it in his 'Idea of Pakistan', "Pakistan is a part-problem and part-solution. An ally in war against terrorism, it is also a potential source of radicalism and nuclear proliferation". The melancholy fact is whatever be the ties of sentiments linking U.S. to India, it is Pakistan which remains a vital ally in the war against terrorism, because the threat to United States and U.S. position in Afghanistan stem from Pakistani society, which only a Pakistan state alone can control. Thus Washington has no option but to work with Pakistan in short run, but it has to take note of Pakistan's deeper malaise, and adopt a policy of "*cooperation that encompasses a strong dose of prevention*".

Initially, Musharraf's rule was welcomed by many Pakistanis as a relief from corrupt politicians, but now it is seen in a different light. There is widespread and well-informed criticism of the army rule. General Zia during his martial law regime was widely despised but army was held in high esteem. But after nearly five years of Musharraf's rule his popularity and also that of the army has diminished and his position is criticized even within the army. His sticking to Army Chief's position implies that no one else can be trusted.

Pakistan's army is still secular, but its officer cadre is becoming anti-American and more "*Islamic*" than it was three decades ago. Many officers are openly supportive of Islamic forces and groups. There are strong links between army and various Islamic groups, especially among retired ISI officers who have joined their former clients. Nineteen retired generals attended the 1991 convention of the Jamaat-I-Islam in Islamabad.

Musharraf has been able like Zia to sidetrack potential rivals and promote officers who are close to him. But there is no guarantee that none of them will step forward to demand Musharraf's removal, if he becomes a liability for army's institutional interests.

4

Talibanization of SWAT Valley—Pakistan's Descent Into Chaos

By allowing imposition of Shariat in the SWAT valley (known as the Switzerland of Pakistan) in the tribal areas of North Western Province, Pakistan Government has abjectly capitulated to the Talibans. Two secular parties of Pakistan, namely, Awami National Party (ANP) and the Peoples' Political Party (PPP) have agreed to this expedient arrangement with a view to buying peace. The deal was signed mainly because the provincial government was concerned about the security of its members and supporters. The ANP has lost about 100 people and could not stand up to the pressure any more.

Taliban militants in the valley led by notorious Mohammad Fazlullah, have terrorized the valley. Schools have been torched as a part of campaign against female education and the aid workers running immunization programmes have been chased away by the militants. Amnesty International estimated that between 2,50,000 and 5,00,000 people have fled their homes since 2007 when Taliban revolt began in the valley.

Pakistan army has not tried to seriously fight the militants on the ground for a variety of reasons. It is either unwilling or unable to go on an all out drive against the Talibans and regain control of vast tracts of territories in the North Western Province. It fears that it will risk its unity if it bitterly fights against the ideological allies and does not want to be sucked into a situation which forces it to launch a massive military action against its own people.

Pakistan Government has now cut a deal with the Cleric Sufi Mohammad who is looked upon as a moderate face of the Talibans. Cleric Sufi Mohammad who himself does not believe in democracy and propagates worldwide Islamic rule has agreed to discuss peace with the militants led by his son-in-law Mohammad Fazlullah. The Cleric was to convince the militants to stop fighting in exchange of imposition of Islamic law and suspension of military offensive. However, Fazlullah, as reported in the Press, has only agreed to temporary ceasefire and not permanent peace.

The official argument that Shariat could not be dictated by the Talibans, but would be the age-old system that ran SWAT till 1969. This reasoning, however, does not explain Fazlullah's militant actions. There are dividends for him and the Taliban such as his *madrasas* being turned into an Islamic university where the Talibans will be allowed to teach. The deal in fact raises a lot of doubt about who will define the Shariat and who will be the neutral arbiter in case of conflict between government's vision of Shariat and the Taliban's conceptualization.

It is, however, very doubtful if the militants will agree to honour this peace deal. A journalist of Pakistan channel ZIO TV, covering peace talks between Maulana Sufi and his son-in-law was shot dead in Matta in SWAT, the stronghold of Fazlullah. He was the second journalist to be murdered by the suspected Islamist, during the last two months. However, a small window to withdraw from the deal has been kept open by the Pakistan Government. According to the Information Minister, Sherry Rehman, President Zardari would sign the accord only after peace prevails.

Western officials as well as many security analysts fear that this lull will not last and this policy of appeasement will further go to embolden the Talibans. They view it as a negative development. US *special envoy to Pakistan Richard Holbrooke said that, the US was troubled and confused about what happened to SWAT because it was not an 'encouraging trend'*. He cautioned against the area being ceded to *'bad guys'*. NATO and European Union have also criticized the accord and both fear that the situation in the SWAT would further worsen.

Taliban's influence started soaring in Pakistan after the fall of the Taliban regime in Afghanistan. Thousands of Talibans fighters fleeing the bombardments of *Tora Bora* caves in eastern Afghanistan crossed over unguarded mountains and disappeared in vast wilderness of tribal areas in Pakistan. There were not enough U.S. troops to cover all the escape routes. And in many cases, Pakistani soldiers looked the other way as foreign fighters crossed over to Pakistan. ISI also provided safe passage to the fugitives.

In Pakistan, President Musharraf under U.S. pressure cracked down on the Al-Qaeda fugitives, but adopted a soft and duplicitous policy towards Talibans. He wanted to use them in due course as strategic assets in Afghanistan and also in Kashmir.

But very soon after successful invasion of Afghanistan U.S. embarked upon plans to invade Iraq, which clearly had no links with Al-Qaeda. This convinced Pakistan's military leaders that U.S. was not serious about long-term commitment to Karzai's regime. This led them to keep Taliban in reserve to be used for reinstating a pro-Pakistani regime in Afghanistan once American interest had turned elsewhere and Karzai regime left to crumble.

Mullah Omar was kept in an ISI safe house in the town of Quetta while his militia was camped in Pastoonabad, a sprawling Quetta suburb. Gulbuddin Hikmetyar, the leader of the radical Muslim militia Hizb-e-Islami was lured back from exile in Iran and allowed to operate freely outside Peshawar, while Jalaluddin Haqqani one of the most violent Taliban commanders, was given sanctuary by the ISI in North Waziristan, a part of FATA. In order to keep contact with such groups beyond the radar of western intelligence, the ISI created a clandestine organization staffed with former ISI trainers and retired Pastoon officers from the army who trained, armed and supported Taliban, in camps outside and around Quetta.

But the Frankenstein monster turned against the Pakistan Government. After the fall of Red Mosque near Islamabad, a wave of retaliatory attacks and suicide bombings swept across North-Western Frontier Province.

Hundreds of suicide bombers born out of the rubble of Red Mosque turned against the Pakistan authorities. Al-Qaeda and Taliban forces now turned attention from Afghanistan to Pakistan where it saw a demoralized army, terrified citizenry and a wonderful opportunity to destabilize the state.

Indeed, Pakistan is now facing a civil war. President Zardari was correct in pointing out that emboldened Talibans now threaten the very existence of Pakistan. Today eight years after 9/11 Mullah Omar and the original Taliban Sura live in Baluchistan province and Taliban tribal leaders live further north in FATA. The fact has to be borne in mind that Talibans belong to neither Afghanistan nor Pakistan but they constitute the lumpen population, the products of refugee camps and militarized *madrasas* and lack of opportunities in the borderlands of Pakistan and Afghanistan.

Hussain Haqqani, the Pakistan Ambassador in U.S.A., has tried to explain the pact as an attempt to drive a wedge between Al-Qaeda and militant Talibans. This is, according to him, a part of a pragmatic military and political strategy to turn our native population against the terrorists and to marginalize the terrorists. This optimism is ill-founded. There are no guarantees that the Talibans will give up the battle easily as many find that they have succeeded in manipulating the state.

The sole option for Pakistan, as the Chairman of the Human Rights Commission of Pakistan I.E. Rehman says "*is to separate the Shariat lobby from the terrorists and creating FATA and PATA as Shariat zones*". However, the question remains if Pakistan can contain the pro-Shariat forces within the frontier region. It will be very hard for the government to insulate the Punjab from the inroads of the militants. The religious extremists already have strong bases across the province and powerful sympathizers in all areas.

Though, Pakistan may not be facing an imminent threat of take-over by Islamic fundamentalists, but there is a real danger of fragmentation with radical Islamists controlling parts of the country. The growing influence of militant Islam in the strategically located North-Western Province and the Western Province of Baluchistan are ominous portents. This is a matter of very grave concern for India as well as the international community. U.S. led war on terror, Pakistan's army's cooperation with militant groups and its stubborn refusal to strengthen democratic institutions has intensified social, ethnic and religious differences in Pakistani society. These are the fault lines from which a geopolitical earthquake could erupt some time which will vastly complicate the regional security situation.

5

Tough Love: U.S. and Pakistan Lock Horns over War on Terror

Recently, in a display of defiance Pakistan rejected as incomplete at least 180 U.S. visa requests. U.S. embassy in Islamabad has now publicly complained that its diplomats are being harassed by Pakistani authorities. The complaint was made with reference to security checks on U.S. diplomatic vehicles introduced by Pakistani Government last month. In a tit-for-tat response Washington has threatened to cut annual Pakistani development assistance worth $ 1.5 billion. These developments indicate growing tensions between two allies jointly fighting the war against terror. Last month even Pentagon admitted that relationship between the two countries is getting increasingly fraught with resentment, miscommunication and mistrust.

Since September 11, 2001, U.S. has given Pakistan $ 11 billion to help it to fight terrorism. The Bush Administration did not demand any accounting of funds. America, however started feeling that it got very little for this investment. American officials have made clear that this time Pakistan will be held accountable for the U.S. Aid that it receives. Analysts say that relations before the two countries really soured when Richard Hallbrooke, US administration's special envoy to Pakistan and Afghanistan, as well as other senior officials publicly suggested that there are elements in Pakistan's all-powerful intelligence services, the ISI, who hold close links with the Talibans. Earlier, Washington's introduction of stiff conditions on funding to the Pakistan army in $ 7.5 billion aid package known as the Kerry-Luger Bill prompted very hostile reaction from among the top military brass in Islamabad.

Now US has stepped up its pressure on the Pakistani army to launch a new offensive against the militants in North Waziristan region from where Taliban affiliated militants are fighting the US led troops in neighbouring Afghanistan. Pakistan's military chief Asaf Kayani has reportedly told General David Petraeus, the head of the US Central Command, that no major military operations are planned any time soon in North Waziristan.

North Waziristan is the sanctuary for important Taliban network known as the Haqqani network run by Jallaludin Haqqani and his son Siraj. According to military officials Siraj fighters pose biggest threat, to the US forces in the eastern part of the Afghanistan. Pakistani officials have expressed their unwillingness to go after Siraj Haqqani who has been an asset for Pakistan's strategic security agencies. Some of them are of the view that Haqqani might find himself in power once the Americans leave Afghanistan. According to *New York Times*, the US officials last month warned the heads of Pakistani intelligence services that if it does not act more forcefully against the Taliban on its own soil the *United States will.* The message was delivered by the National Security Advisor General, James Jones and White House counter-terrorism chief John Brennan.

After the loss of their centre of gravity in South Waziristan the militants appeared to have relocated themselves in North Waziristan and from there began to radiate their war of terror again. In South Waziristan Pakistan military have been able to recapture the territory but failed to capture either the militants or their ammunition. Pakistan army has experienced little or no resistance from the militants as all the armed men had left the area well in advance. Crucially, not a single important Taliban commander or foreign militant has been killed or arrested since the launch of operations on October 17, 2009. The militants fleeing the South Waziristan operation have dispersed to *Mohmand, Khybar, Orakzai* and *Bazaur* agencies from where they have launched a wave of suicide bombings inside the North-Western Province.

The well-known Pakistani newspaper *Dawn* in an editorial (3rd January, 2010) says that North Waziristan, the new terrorism central, must and can be reclaimed by the state from the militants and this is being recognized also by the security establishment, albeit privately at this point. *Miranshah,* the headquarters of North Waziristan is a very lucrative smuggling route, something the locals are loath to give up to fight a potentially unwinnable war against the state.

Further signs of solidarity between Pakistani and Afghan Taliban are surfacing. The suicide blast by a Jihadi triple agent in Afghanistan on December 30 that killed 7 American spies was a calamity for the CIA. A video later on released showed that the bomber, a Jordanian doctor, was delivering his farewell message besides the chief of Pakistani Taliban Hakimullah Mahsud who fled south Waziristan and joined hands with Afghan Talibans in North Waziristan. The blurring of militant groups may persuade the Pakistan army that an offensive in North Waziristan is unavoidable.

Drone Attacks

America has intensified drone attacks inside Pakistan. A number of such attacks during the last two weeks had taken place in North Waziristan tribal region, illustrating Obama administration's increasing reliance on this tactic, despite official protests from Islamabad. Drone attacks had so far killed 10 senior Al-Qaeda leaders since 2008 and some 300 civilians in the past two years. The drone attacks had also ignited anti-American sentiments among the Pakistanis. US Senator and Chairman of the Arms Services Committee, Curl Levin, has rebuked the Pakistani leadership and said that the vocal criticism, of the drone strike is unacceptable when in private they understand and support the drone attacks. Washington would prefer a silence on their part rather than a public criticism, which creates animosity between the Pakistani public and the USA. So long the drone strikes have been limited to Pakistan's Pashtoon tribal regions near the Afghan border, but an expansion of strike under consideration could involve missile attacks on Quetta where the Taliban leader Mullah Omar is suspected to be hiding.

Well-known American expert on Pakistan Stephen Cohen says that American strategy has somewhat changed towards Pakistan and he characterized it as "*tough-love*". America will be tough with people and groups who are America's enemies and also Pakistan's enemies. In the present scenario, United States needs Pakistan to continue successfully its expanding war in Afghanistan and Pakistan also cannot do without the United States. There is always a fear that any massive reorganization of US strategy will lead to the collapse of the Pakistan as a democratic state and none in US wants it. Indeed, for more than a decade Pakistan has negotiated with US with a gun on its own head. It has held out the threat that if the present establishment collapses Jihadis will takeover. The threat of Jihadi takeover is the ultimate American nightmare and Pakistan has adroitly played on this American fear. The hard fact however is that many of the Jihadis are in uniform.

There is now a growing fear that Laskar-e-Toiba (LeT) together with Al-Qaeda will seek to provoke confrontation between India and Pakistan by launching another terror strike like that of 26/11. Robert Gates, US Defence Secretary voiced this fear and said that the "syndicate of terror" comprising LeT, Taliban and Al-Qaeda constitute a serious threat to the security of entire area.

6

Insidious Spread: Talibanization of Pakistan

Pakistan army has at long last launched offensives against the Taliban forces in North-Western Frontier Province. The offensives in Buner and lower Dir provinces have resulted in bombardment of Taliban positions and death of a number of Taliban militants. Pakistan top military commanders have also reportedly pledged to extend maximum support to the civilian government in tackling militancy with "*zero tolerance*". General David Petraeus, Commander of US Central Command, has told US officials that he hoped to see concrete action by the Pakistan Government in the next two weeks to destroy the Talibans.

Earlier, Pakistani authorities had abjectly capitulated before the Talibans at SWAT and agreed to the imposition of Shariat in the SWAT valley. It was an expedient arrangement to buy peace and this policy of appeasement only emboldened the Talibans who, contrary to the agreement, did not lay down their arms and tried to project themselves in the adjoining districts. Security analysts fear that SWAT area will become another "*emirate from which a wider Talibanization campaign can be launched*".

The noted Pakistani columnist, Ayaz Amir, a former Pakistani Army officer and now a Parliamentarian said the justification that "*Nizam-e-Adil regulation will bring peace to SWAT and its environs was hollow. We had acquiesced in a great act of surrender Munich is written all over it*". (*The News*, April 7, 2009)

Emboldened Talibans led by Baitullah Mehsud attacked the Sri Lankan Cricket Team at Lahore and followed it up by launching another attack at Police Training School near Lahore. Mehsud threatened more serious strikes in different cities with a view to forcing the government to stop cooperating with the United States in the war against terror. The Jihadis thus sent a clear signal that they are well entrenched inside Pakistan and not merely across the country's western border.

President, Asif Ali Zardari has exhorted his people to give full support to the military and demonstrate the will to keep Pakistan as a moderate, modern and democratic state. However, there are doubts whether Pakistani army will go all out against the Talibans to crush them. There is every likelihood that it may soon enter, as it has done on many occasions earlier, into some peace deals with the Talibans.

The trouble is that Pakistan army's senior officers still hold the view that they would be in a position to control the militants and use them as per their requirements. In a taped conversation between General Parvez Musharraf and Mohd, Aziz Khan, the then Chief of the General Staff, which India released in 1999, Aziz said that the army had the Jihadis by the "*tooti*" (privates). Now to their dismay they find that the Islamists are following their own agenda. They are sending suicide bombers to attack members of the Pakistan religious minorities and political leaders and even ISI Headquarters at camp Hamza itself as acts of revenge for Pakistan's support for American war against terror and attack by Pakistan's army on Taliban's strongholds at FATA. Groups like Laskar-e-Toiba, Jaish-i-Muhammad which were originally created by the ISI to help Pakistan in an asymmetric proxy war against India have joined hands with the Talibans. As Taliban comes under increasing pressure due to attacks by American drones, it is joining Punjabi groups to launch terrorist attacks across the Punjab's heartland at will. Bruce Riedel who led the Obama administrations recently completed strategy review of Pakistan and Afghanistan said that there has been a "*coalescence of the militant groups*". Connections that have already existed are becoming tighter and more public than in the past. Like Musharraf, his successor General Kiyani has pretended to deal firmly with the extremists, but retained in actual practice army's links with the Jihadis and Talibans for strategic depth in Afghanistan and for bleeding India.

US President, Barak Obama during his speech marking 100 days in office said that Pakistan's obsession with India as the mortal threat has been misguided and the Pakistan army has started to take Taliban threat more seriously. There is some recognition that the biggest threat to Pakistan comes internally. However, it will not be easy for Pakistani army to set aside doctrines and preparations that had been developed over generations. It is indeed going to be a tough call. There is an all-pervasive fear in Pakistani army that the United States may simply lose interest in Afghanistan once it captures the leadership of Al-Qaeda (as the US did after the Soviet withdrawal from Afghanistan), leaving Pakistan exposed to Indian encirclement. There is also a strong belief in the army that both USA and India are destabilizing FATA and rest of the country as a prelude to depriving Pakistan of its nuclear weapons. They see India through tinted lens and fear that US might choose India over Pakistan.

There is no immediate threat of Talibans taking over Pakistan but they are extending their influence in non-Pashtoon areas through sleeper cells and various sub rosa activities. The Mohazir movement chief Altaf Hussain repeatedly warns of Talibanization of Karachi. Serious clashes between Pashtoon and Mohazirs are now erupting in Karachi resulting in immense loss of human lives and properties. In a testimony to the Pakistani National Assembly Standing Committee, NWFP police chief Malik Navid stated that Taliban was spreading almost in every area of Pakistan, especially to cities like Lahore and Karachi. Their aim is to create seamless web of cells spreading from NWFP and Waziristan to Southern Punjab and Karachi.

President Obama expressed the hope that Pakistan's nuclear weapons will not fall in the hands of the militants and America can make sure that Pakistan's nuclear weapons remain secure primarily because US and Pakistan have strong military-to-military consultation and cooperation. It means that America has some understanding of Pakistan army regarding the safety of the nukes. For imminent threats of seizure by the militants, some contingency plans have perhaps been kept ready.

Pakistan's case is perhaps somewhat unique because control and decision making regarding the nuclear weapons is solely in the hands of the military despite the constitutional provision of inclusion of the civilians in nuclear decision-making. Another important feature of Pakistan's nuclear infrastructure is that much of it from the outset have been deployed in the west of Pakistan to extend warning time of possible Indian attacks. The unintended consequence is the location of much of the nuclear infrastructure to the volatile region to the west and to the north-west of Islamabad where the militants are now calling the shots. Pakistan's Khusab reactors are situated on the border of the Punjab and North-West Frontier Province, now the scene of heavy fighting between Talibans and government forces. Another vulnerable facility is Gadwal Uranium Enrichment Plant less than 60 miles south of Buner district, which has, of late, witnessed fierce clashes between the Talibans and the government troops. US can remove the weapons in the event of an extreme emergency or civil war only with agreement and cooperation of the Pakistani army or a pro-western part of it.

The head of Pakistan nuclear programme, General Khalid Kidwai has declared that their security arrangements are foolproof. Any attempt to get the nuclear weapons by surprise, stealth or force would be a high-risk affair and trigger a very hostile reaction within Pakistan itself. However, far greater danger is the radicalization of

Pakistan military and the possibility of an "*insider job*", i.e. seizure of some part of the arsenal by anti-American radicals within the Pakistan armed force. Another dangerous possibility is the infiltration of the nuclear programme by scientists sympathetic to the militants and dissemination of information by them. A retired CIA official John Brennan has said that Pakistan's nuclear safeguards are robust enough to withstand a fair amount of commotion but none can predict what will happen if the country slides towards civil war. If there are power centres within the army, they will view the strategic arsenal as a real prize. And "*that will be a nightmare scenario*".

7

A Friend and Master

Pakistan is on a perilous path. The country looks more unstable than ever. Lawyers' agitation has now taken the form of a strong popular movement for restoration of democracy. It is a stirring outburst of the democratic yearnings of the people of Pakistan. There is enormous public sympathy and support for the suspended Chief Justice Iftikhar Choudhary. On March 9, 2007, in the presence of six other uniformed Generals at his Army Headquarters in Rawalpindi General Musharraf ordered Choudhary to resign. The judge had upset him and his colleagues and gave a number of populist rulings against the government. He also audaciously demanded investigation into cases of disappearance mostly from his native place Baluchistan where an insurgency is flickering. This was an unprecedented event in Pakistan where a civilian was telling a bullying general where to get off. Chowdhary enthusiastically supported by the lawyers in the country has now become a hero of the democratic forces in Pakistan. In Pakistan judiciary was diminished by repeatedly endorsing extra constitutional interventions and pledging oaths to military coup-makers. Only now it is recovering some of its prestige.

On May 12, 2007, Chowdhary and his supporters were attacked by a mob in Karachi where they had gone to address a meeting. A number of people were killed in the violence that erupted in the city. The killings in Karachi were different from terrorist attacks as it was carried out by the supporters of Karachi's disreputable ruling party, (MQM) forming part of the weak national coalition through which Musharraf rules. Though Musharraf feels scared and beleaguered, this enkindling of a democratic movement in Pakistan should be a cause of celebration. It is a democratic outburst after nearly seven years under army rule. Many political observers strongly feel that for fighting terrorism in Pakistan strong democratic institutions are needed. Pakistan's future is linked with the restoration of democracy and supremacy of the constitution and not with the military dictatorship.

Musharraf has now issued a statement containing veiled threats of extra-constitutional measures to save the situation. He knows that though he may get the current Parliament elect him as President in September, but he also knows that the Supreme Court may hold it as unconstitutional and this move may rebound on him. He also further knows that in a free and fair election even without the participation of Bhutto and Nawaz Sharif, he and his party is bound to lose.

In this difficult and trying time for Musharraf, America has come forward to extend support to his military regime. The statement of Nicholas Burns, American Under Secretary, indicates that U.S. continues to support General Musharraf for a host of reasons and wants him around for the foreseeable future. But his statement also indicates that Musharraf's strategy to help the U.S. in the war against terror is not working very well. U.S. expects him to "*do more*" and he needs to build greater political capacity at home by democratising society and welcoming new and liberal political allies in the government. This means that U.S. is not likely to support extra constitutional measures by General Musharraf because such methods would isolate him and deepen political crisis instead of enhancing his capacity and stabilizing his polity. U.S. has also cautioned Musharraf on media curbs and reversing advances towards greater freedom of the press. The State Department spokesman Sean McCormack said that a Pakistan Government has to come to terms with new freedoms that had emerged in Pakistani society concerning the freedom of expression and media as well. It bears recall that General Musharraf decreed new powers to the Pakistan Electronic Media Regulatory Authority (PEMRA) allowing it to seal the offices of television and radio broadcasters, seize equipments and suspend operating licences. There was widespread outrage and the General was forced to suspend the ordinance until a committee had reviewed it.

Bush administration so far has always backed Musharraf and viewed him as a reliable ally in war against terrorism. It has provided to Pakistan $ 10 billion as aid since 9/11 as part of the war against terrorism and this security assistance is channelled through Pakistan's army. Congress is also considering Bush administration's request for additional 100 million dollars for economic aid to Pakistan's Federally Administered Tribal areas.

U.S. support for Pakistan is grounded on a number of factors. First, U.S.A. does not want to see Pakistan in the grip of chaos and uncertainty. Musharraf so far has been an useful ally in the war against Al-Qaeda. There is fear that the ouster of Musharraf may bring some other leaders who may not offer equal cooperation. Pakistan's cooperation is essential, particularly at a time when troops of America and its NATO allies are battling against the Talibans in Afghanistan and trying to set-up there a viable government. Second, there is anxiety that the current unrest may lead to a takeover of Pakistan Government by the terrorists. Third, there is concern over nuclear weapon's leakage. There is fear that the terrorists taking advantage of prolonged instability may be able to steal or seize Pakistan's nuclear weapons or fissile materials.

However, many expert analysts are of the view that these fears are somewhat unfounded. According to a strategic analyst Alex Stloar Pakistan army's Strategic Plan Division devotes over nearly 8000 men, mostly undercover, to protect Pakistan's fissile materials. Pakistan's military is capable and professional and it is highly improbable that it would hand over its "*crown jewels*" to individuals and organisations that it cannot control during a period of unrest. Similarly, the fear that the current unrest could lead to a takeover of the Pakistani Government by the extremist elements is also misplaced. Though religious parties are an important element in Pakistani society, but till now their political clout remains limited and it is unlikely that they could engineer a takeover of the Pakistan Government as they lack popular support and military power. Further, if

Musharraf's presidency loses its credibility, the military may judge him to be a liability and replace him. However, any new army leadership will be mindful of American stakes in the region. The military has no desire to lose the material benefits of its close relationship with U.S.A. nor does it want to push U.S.A. towards closer strategic relationship with India.

Amidst growing turbulence in unstable nuclear-armed Pakistan experts are questioning the U.S. administration's reliance on Pakistan's military alone to provide a moderating of pro-western influence. In a blistering editorial *New York Times* observed that "*more unpopular Pakistan's military dictator Pervez Musharraf becomes at home, and less he is willing to fight the Talibans, the more Bush administration clings to him*". In a recently held conference hosted by the Hudson Institute, Washington some well-known experts differing in terms of their nationality, political orientation and analytical perspective emphasised the need for a review of the American policy towards Pakistan. Marvin G. Weinbam, a scholar at the Middle East Institute in Washington, describes Pakistan's contribution to regional counter-terrorism efforts as "*inconsistent, incomplete and at times insincere*". The speakers strongly felt the need for U.S. to adopt measures to promote return of civilian rule in Pakistan or risk polarizing Pakistan's politics between Islamic extremists and the military. American policy makers must recognise that "*there is more to Pakistan than Musharraf*" and pay more attention to the dysfunctional state of Pakistan. Democratic Committee Chairperson, Gary Ackerman at a hearing of the South-Asia and Middle East sub-committee in the House of Representatives said that riots over Musharraf's decision to remove the country's Chief Justice highlights the fact that the return of Pakistan's democracy is an issue that has "*slipped in emphasis if not actual importance*" and Washington should have "*more than one phone number to dial in Pakistan*". Hussain Haqqani, Director of the Centre of International Relations of Boston University, in the same hearing also expressed misgivings about the personalization of relations between the world's sole superpower and nuclear armed Pakistan and felt that this is not the best way forward for either. It does not even fulfil the short-term purpose of securing Pakistan's cooperation in the global war on terror.

It is not known if General Musharraf will be able to ride out the gathering storm. It seems that he is living out his fading days of power. But the U.S. policy-makers have to bear in mind that prolongation of army rule will cause further institutional erosion in Pakistan. It will be a geo-strategic calamity if Pakistan becomes a failed state, generating enormous uncertainty in the entire region. Thus, for U.S. policy-makers military rulers of Pakistan are becoming more a problem than a solution.

8

Army will continue to call the Shots in Pakistan

President, Pervez Musharraf in his address to the nation after the Army crackdown on Lal Masjid has vowed to eliminate terrorism from every nook and corner of the country. It is estimated that storming of Lal Masjid by the Pakistani military commandos resulted in a loss of 103 lives. His bold action against Islamic radicals and clerics has been appreciated by his western allies. President Bush has lauded his role in the war against terrorism and appreciated his policy of "*enlightened moderation*". But many opposition parties particularly, Mutahida Mazalis-e-Amal (MMA), an alliance of religious parties as well as leaders like Imran Khan have denounced him as an American stooge.

Lal Masjid action has also triggered a violent reaction from various militant outfits and right wing political parties. They have threatened that bloodshed at Lal Masjid will only usher in an Islamic revolution in Pakistan. Suicide attacks by the terrorists in different areas of Pakistan have taken a heavy toll of lives and properties. They have targeted on police and the security forces. It is too early to predict the impact of the storming of Lal Masjid on

Musharraf's future. Moderate Pakistani support his decisive, though somewhat belated move, but many of those who support the government action nevertheless insist that the militants should have been given safe passage in order to save the lives of women and children. Anti-Musharraf politicians are trying to exploit the situation and hoping that Musharraf will not survive the crisis. The only divergent view is that of Benazir Bhutto who justified the operation but cunningly qualified it by adding that religious extremism is a consequence of the army rule and only civilian supremacy in a democracy can counter it effectively.

In this troublous time American support will strengthen Musharraf's hands, though it may make him more unpopular. Many American strategists and policy-makers feel that Musharraf's counter-terrorism measures are "*insincere and incomplete*" but the official U.S. policy will continue to be in favour of supporting Musharraf and the Army. There are sound reasons behind it.

The real problem in Pakistan is that it has become a dysfunctional state. Provincial governors, local commanders and rich landlords have become power unto themselves and the Central Government can claim limited authority over the country. The only institution that works in Pakistan is Army, which by and large, is professional and competent. It also swallows up 39 per cent of the government budget. In a recent book, the author Ayesha Siddiqui has detailed the vast holdings of Pakistan's "*military economy*" including banks, schools, universities and companies are worth $ 10 billion. The all-powerful army with or without Musharraf will continue to shape and influence in a big way Pakistan's strategic policy. Daniel Markey, in a perceptive article in the journal *Foreign Affairs (July-August 2007)* points out that Pakistan's civilian leaders always had to negotiate a working relationship which the army in which the army generals always held the whiphand and retained a significant decision making power. Pakistan's civilian leaders, regardless of party affiliations, will have to accept this reality. Again even if it withdraws from politics, army will remain an essential element in Pakistan's fight against terrorism. Pakistan's post-independence history shows that the army always called the shots even during the period of civilian rule and had its decisive voice in all foreign policy and national security issues including Pakistan's nuclear programmes and relations with Jihadi groups in Afghanistan and Kashmir. Benazir Bhutto when she was the Prime Minister remained, by all accounts, in the dark about country's nuclear programmes. Under Musharraf, the tentacles of the army have further spread and it has become much more deeply entrenched in country's economy and politics. It will be difficult, if not impossible, to sideline or marginalize it in foreseeable future. Now, as Pakistan is facing the full blast of terrorist violence, army will remain the most important element in the war against terror.

Army Mullah Nexus

During the cold war and until 9/11, U.S.A. winked at Pakistan army's close association with the Jihadis. In regard to Kashmir, Washington used to criticize India more for human rights violations by its security forces than Pakistan for aiding and abetting the "*freedom fighters*". In Afghanistan, U.S.A. and Pakistan were partners in helping the Mujahideens in their anti-Soviet operations. But 9/11 brought about a sea change in the situation. With counter-terrorism becoming the top priority in the agenda of the White House, Islamabad's semantic distinction between freedom-fighters and terrorists no longer held water. In this "*with us or against us*" era Musharraf was forced to snap links with the Talibans in Afghanistan and reduce full sponsorship of the militants operating in Kashmir. Musharraf's close association with U.S.A.'s counter-terrorism campaign has made him the first target of the terrorists. There were three attempts on his life and he escaped death on each occasion by a whisker. Now, the deputy of Osama-Bin-Laden, Aymen Jawahiri has given a call to the militants to kill Musharraf.

It is a fact that in the army and ISI there are elements who have retained their old Taliban links. Deep in Pakistan army's psyche is the fear that U.S.A. may abandon Pakistan as it had done in 1990s after the Soviets were driven out of Afghanistan. U.S.A. may do it again after Pakistan's strategic utility is over. Pakistan's army generals also feel worried over India and America coming close together. So by threatening to abandon or cutting off support or aid, Washington would confirm the suspicions of the army generals that U.S.A.'s interests in Pakistan are selfish and cynical and Pakistan should be prepared to traverse a lonely path and live without U.S. aid. Washington's coercive leverage, as Danial Markey correctly points out, is limited by the fact that both Islamabad and Washington know that U.S.A. has lot to loose by cutting off Pakistan. If Washington acts tough, Pakistan's army can sabotage in a big way American policy against Al-Qaeda throughout the region. One reason as to why the Pakistan army has retained its ties with Talibans is that they want to keep open "it *post American option to constrain what they fear a pro-Indian Government in Kabul*".

Even if now army because of mounting criticism or after the elections goes back to the barrack, political and religious extremism in Pakistan cannot be countered by divided and indisciplined political parties without army's active support. Undiluted civilian democracy without army backing, "*will be a recipe of anarchy*". A civilian leader, however influential and charismatic when he comes to power will have to be sensitive to army's institutional interest. Fareed Zakaria tellingly points out in an article in *Newsweek* that back in 18th century fedrick the Great's Prussia was characterised as "*not a state with army but an army with a state*". This perhaps is the complex reality with Pakistan.

There is a silverlining to the Lal Masjid show down. Optimists hope that it will force the Army to end its alliances with religious forces and see the dangers posed by the Jihadis who have made desperate attempts to derail the peace process with India, assassinate Musharraf, Talibanize frontier regions and enforce Shariat laws in the nation's capital.

Pakistan's history shows that military rule tends to strengthen the extremists. It is a fact that, though in a less blatant way than the previous military ruler Zia-ul-Haq, Musharraf made himself a patron of the militants. With army's backing, Islamists have tasted power in two of Pakistan's four provinces, North-Western Province and Baluchistan, and meanwhile in the lawless tribal areas bordering on Afghanistan a "*Pakistani Taliban*" has sprouted.

An enlightened moderate politico-military alliance is necessary to stem the tide of terrorism in Pakistan. Washington has understood the need to shift the gears and not reverse the course. It wants to carry the twin policy of supporting the Pakistan army and promoting democracy. Thus, while standing by the army generals U.S.A. is pressing for a free and fair election in Pakistan. It fears that without external pressure hardliners around Musharraf will be tempted to rig the election as they did in 2002 and 2005. U.S.A. is also exerting pressure on Musharraf to cut a deal with Bhutto's PPP to form a united government with a moderate electoral base. Washington will not press for Musharraf's ouster, but will seek to prevail upon the army to disengage from domestic politics. It is reported that Musharraf's men are now holding discussions with Benazir Bhutto as to how to divide power between them. But all this will be possible only after the election. Meanwhile, after Pakistan Supreme Court's direction to set aside Musharraf's order on suspension of the Chief Justice, there is strident demand by the opposition parties for his resignation. However, it seems unlikely that the general is going to oblige. It will also mean an unacceptable loss of face for the army.

9

Extension of General Asfaq Parvez Kayani's Tenure: A Bloodless Coup

General Kayani who was completing his 3 year tenure as Chief of Army Staff (COAS) has now been given another three years extension by the Pakistani Prime Minister, Yousuf Raza Gilani. He will now be COAS till November 28, 2013. While announcing the decision to give an extension, the Prime Minster, Gilani said that the extension had been given in the interest of continuity at a time when Pakistani army was continuing operations against the elements who want to impose 'a system of their choice in the country'. *(an apparent reference to Tehrik-Taliban).*

The three year extension of Kayani's tenure is the second incident in Pakistan's history when a civilian regime extended the tenure of the COAS. The first such extension was given by former President, Iskandar Mirza to General Ayub Khan. Subsequently, the three army chiefs, namely, General Ayub Khan, Zia-ul-Haq and Musharraf had extended their own terms. The rumour of the bloodless coup had been doing the rounds in Islamabad for some time. Many Pakistanis view Kayani's extension as a "topi drama" (drama enacted by the people who wear the beret), an attempt by the army to make People believe that the democracy is in place and decisions are taken by a democratic government. It is well known that Kayani was writing his own orders. In the last two years, Kayani could have overthrown the elected government and established martial law whenever he wanted. Close on the heels of three years extension granted to General Kayani, the U.S. Government announced its decision to retain its ambassador to Pakistan, Anna Patterson for an unspecified period even though she had already spent 4 years in Islamabad.

Kayani has been described as a "soldiers' soldier" by U.S. officials. The U.S. Chairman of the Joint Chiefs of Staff, Mike Moullen is a close friend of General Kayani. The United States has studiously avoided taking a public position, but U.S. diplomats and military officers had indicated noticeable desire to see him at the helm of affairs. Kayani, however, has avoided projecting himself as 'America's Choice'.

In the counter-insurgency operations against TTP, Kayani had partial successes in the SWAT Valley, South Waziristan Bazaur and Orakzai agencies. Army had been able to wrest from Pakistani Talibans, the territorial control of the areas, but has not been able to destroy their capability of launching terrorist strikes in tribal and non-tribal areas. But he has carefully avoided taking action against the Afghan Talibans operating in the tribal areas. He has viewed them as strategic assets in the unfolding scenario in Afghanistan.

Kayani shares the strong and traditional suspicions of India nursed by Punjabi Officers of Pakistan army who view India as a bitter enemy of Pakistan and a graver threat than the Taliban. Musharraf started as a fierce adversary of India, but mellowed down over the years. Kayani shows no signs of mellowing down. He is of the clear view that Pakistan should try to counter India in every possible way whether J. & K. and Afghanistan and elsewhere. He feels like many other officers of the Pakistani army that Pakistan can continue to harass "*soft India*". With nuclear arms and missiles and a tough army, Islamabad can withstand considerable Indian pressure.

The documents made available by an Organization called Wiki Leaks now indicate that Pakistan allowed representatives of the ISI to meet the Talibans in strategy sessions to organize the militant groups to fight American soldiers and Indian interests in Afghanistan. It encouraged Haqanni networks to kill Indians resulting in bomb blast in Indian Embassy in Kabul. General Kayani ran the ISI network from 2004-07, a period from which many of the reports are drawn.

Developments in Afghanistan now have immensely strengthened the position of Pakistan army and hands of General Kayani. Pakistan Army has a feeling that after years of marginalisation, the U.S. needs it more than ever. By making apparent its desperation to leave Afghanistan, Obama administration has provided a sense of indispensability to the Pakistani military. The West can only leave early and save face if it is able to bring moderate Talibans to the negotiating table. ISI which has been a patron of the Talibans for last two decades, therefore becomes a crucial conduit for the West to come to an understanding with the Talibans. Thus, Washington has no choice but keep Pakistan army in good humour. Another reason is geography. America's supply of food, fuel and rations and ammunitions to its troops have to go through Pakistan. Alternative route through Iran is not feasible politically, and route through Central Asia remains to be developed. Pakistanis are extracting geo-strategic rent from the U.S.A.

This undermines India's interest in Afghanistan in a dramatic fashion. The last thing India wants to see is a return of elements of India hating Talibans in reconstituted government in Afghanistan. As Pakistan seizes upper hand in Afghanistan, General Kayani in no mood to talk much less to listen to India. The Pakistan army is playing for high regional stakes. It wants to eradicate India's influence in Afghanistan and regain strategic depth by brokering a settlement which will bring those Afghan Taliban sections to power that it supports. Further developments in India have emboldened Pakistan in hardening its attitude. The growing Naxalites threat, turmoil in Kashmir and constant fear in India of another Mumbai type terror attack have given an impression that India is unable to deal with crucial security issues.

It has been suggested by some strategists that India should deal directly with Pakistan army as they are the real decision makers. The Americans understand this. They prefer to deal directly with the military dealings with the civilian government are only for the sake of form. Indian Foreign Service Officials who deal with Pakistan also know that when they talk with the Pakistan Government, they are actually talking to the army but using a via media. The India policy in Pakistan is directed and scripted by GHQ in Rawalpindi. This has always been the case. Whenever a Prime Minister tried to make his own policy, as Nawaz Sharif did, he had to pay a heavy price.

Unfolding Scenario in Afghanistan remains hazy. According to Henry Kissinger, former Secretary of State of U.S., "*America needs a strategy not an alibi*". It is in America's national interest to prevent Jihadi Islam from gaining additional momentum which it will certainly do if it can claim to have defeated the United States and its allies after overcoming the Soviet Union. A precipitate withdrawal will weaken governments in many countries with significant Islamic minorities. It is being hoped that the United States will be able to turnover the responsibility to an Afghan Government and national Army whose writ runs across the country, and the turnover is to begin next summer. Neither the premise nor the deadline is realistic.

India has now to rethink seriously its policy of peaceful negotiations with Pakistan and should not show any impatience about resumptions of talks. It may not shun talks and but not talk at any cost. It has also to think of fashioning a new bold policy towards Kabul, otherwise it will lose grounds in both Afghanistan and Pakistan.

10

Pakistan's Nuclear Weapons—Security Issues

Prof. Shaun Gregory has reported that in the past five years militants have attacked three Pakistani nuclear facilities/ store houses at Wah, Sargoda air base and Kamran, exposing loopholes in Pakistan's security regime for its nuclear weapons. In August 12, 2008, two suicide bombers attacked the gates of Pakistan ordnance factory wall killing 70 people. It was the deadliest terrorist attack on a nuclear installation in Pakistan's history. On October 24, 2009, 8 people were killed in a suicide attack on Pakistan's air base complex Kamran, which also stores nuclear weapons to be air dropped.

Today Pakistan has world's fastest growing nuclear arsenal. In the last four years, it has expanded from 60-80 warheads to over 110 nuclear weapons. Some in the West believe that Pakistan started preparing nuclear-tipped missiles in the middle of 1999 Kargil war. Pakistan nuclear warheads used the implosion design with a solid core of 15 to 20 kg. of enriched uranium. Pakistan now produces about 100 kg of enriched uranium in a year, but is rapidly expanding its nuclear infrastructure with the help of the China. Pakistan reportedly has several nuclear storage facilities, though their exact locations are not known. They are mainly in the military bases. Although separate storage may provide a layer of protection against accidental launch or prevent seizure of an assembled weapon, it makes easier for unauthorized people to remove the weapons fissile material cores if they are not assembled. When the United States decided to launch attack on Afghan Talibans after September 11, 2001, President, Parvez Musharraf reportedly ordered that Pakistan's nuclear arsenals should be redeployed to at least in "*six secret new locations*." At that time, Islamabad leadership was uncertain whether United States would decide to conduct strikes against Pakistan's nuclear assets if Pakistan did not assist against the Taliban.

Pakistan's nuclear weapons are handled by Pakistani army's Strategic Planning Division (SPD). This force comprises around 12 thousand personnel and it is headed by a Lieutenant General. SPD personnel have to pass Personal Reliability Programme (PRP) and Human Reliability Programme (HRP) before induction. Screenings are reportedly done after every two years and some times randomly. After the A.Q. Khan scandal in 2004, these tests are being applied to senior personnel. The weapons are stored in underground sites with multiple security rings and guarded by big heavily armed SPD personnel. Experts are of the view that physically overwhelming these weapons' sites will be very difficult but a highly plausible scenario is theft of fissile materials or fusing components used in the bomb by radicalized personnel in the SPD.

The pilfered materials could be used as a radiological device or what is called '*dirty bomb*.' It is a conventional explosive used to scatter radioactive materials. It spreads panic rather than inflicting mass casualties. Another possible use for the fissile materials is for building a "*simple implosion devise*" and targets could be an Indian city. Today, Pakistan is feverously producing nuclear weapons as well as fissile materials. The larger the number of weapons, the greater is the threat of leakage.

Previously India and Pakistan used to reassure themselves that neither side could use a nuclear weapon because aggressor would suffer from the fallout. That may no longer hold good after American decision in 2008 gave India civilian technology. This had stimulated Pakistan's decision to strengthen its nuclear arsenal. It has now tested a new mobile missile with a miniaturized nuclear warhead designed to destroy tank formation with little radiation beyond the battlefield. This has also increased the risk that border tensions may escalate into something far more serious and lethal. Pakistani Generals are of the opinion that this tactical weapon would be able to meet the threats of rapid and punitive conventional thrusts by Indian forces against Pakistan.

U.S. officials have so far conveyed confidence in the security of Islamabad's nuclear weapons. American Secretary of Defense, Robert Gates, stated in an interview on January 21, 2010, that U.S. "*is very comfortable with security of Pakistan's nuclear weapons*". But a recent study by Mathew Bunn of Harvard University managing the Atom Project asserts that Pakistan's stockpile "*faces a greater threat from Islamic extremists seizing nuclear weapons than any other nuclear stockpile on earth.*"

According to Davis Albright, a noted nuclear Proliferation analyst, Pakistan's nuclear weapons are not thought to be "*one point safe*" or equipped with Permissive Action Links (PAL) meant to prevent unauthorized use of such weapons. PAL requires an entry code before such weapons can be armed and fired.

Again Pakistan's nuclear assets remain vulnerable for another reason. From the outset, they have been deployed to the west of Pakistan to extend warning time of possible Indian attacks against them and delay overrun from the ground. The nuclear installations in the volatile regions of West and North-West of Islamabad remain exposed to the grave threats from the terrorist groups. In Pakistan control and decision making regarding nuclear weapons, is totally in the hands of the army, despite periods of civilian rule. Former Prime Ministers of Pakistan, Benazir Bhutto and Nawaz Sharif are on record stating that were clearly out of the decision making loop with regard to nuclear weapons.

Unfortunately, Pakistan army is no longer a loyal professional and disciplined force as it was thought to be. The "*beard counts*" in the army has increased. Many young officers of post-*Zia-ul-Haq* era have been radicalized. There is also a growing feeling among sections of the army that they are fighting against their own countrymen at the behest of U.S.A. It is reported in *New York Times* that the Army Chief General Kayani is under pressure from anti American, radicalized lower and middle ranks of the army for not adopting a tough line against U.S. Reports of 'Colonels' coup may be overstated. However, if there is a collapse of command and control situation, and emergence of different power centres within the army, each will view the strategic arsenal as a real prize and that will be in every sense a nightmare scenario.

11

Punjabi Talibans—Monster Turns on Master

On May 28, 2010, there was massacre of over one hundred worshippers at two mosques in Lahore by Pakistani militants. The worshippers belong to Ahmedia sect, one of the religious minorities that Pakistan discriminates against or declines to adequately protect. The Ahmedias are regarded as heretics for believing that Mohammad was not the last prophet. According to police sources Punjabi Taliban groups is behind this massacre. Later on, they also carried out an audacious attack on a hospital in order to free one of the captured terrorists who was receiving treatment there. Though they did not succeed, they killed four policemen and a patient before escaping. The victims of two mosques included a retired Army Lt. General and several old Judges and Civil Servants.

In the past, Punjabi militants have been somewhat distinct from the militants from the tribal areas and remained under some form of control of the Pakistan armed forces. The Punjabi Talibans are now running out of control. The growing role of Punjabis marks a major escalation of the extremist threats in Pakistan. Punjab is the heartland of Pakistan and home to its political and military elite. Many Punjabi Taliban leaders have received military training which make them more lethal than rural Pashtoon fighters. Pakistan is now witnessing coalescence of various militant Jihadi groups. According to Bruce Riedl, a former top official in the White House National Security Council dealing with South Asia, the big danger is that these groups are fighting for recruits from same Punjabi families and clans that the Pakistani army recruits for its *"Officer Corps"*.

Southern Punjab has become a hub for Punjabi militants who maintain close touch with the Talibans and travel to the tribal belt for both training and combat. The traffic is in fact two way with Punjabi Militants providing safe haven to Taliban fighters and commanders when needed. Indeed, Taliban movement in Pakistan is now dominated by Punjabi militant groups once created and controlled by ISI. Now like a Frankenstein monster these groups have joined Al-Qaeda and Taliban to battle the Pakistani Government. Their goal is to spread the message of rigid intolerant Islam to the heartland of Pakistan and beyond. Militants' goals have become increasingly maximalist. Many seek just not to liberate Kashmir but see eventual control of territory within India as the true prize of their struggle. Nasar Javed, a Lashkar-e-Toiba official, delivering a speech at Kuba Mosque, in Islambad in February 5, 2008 declared that "The Government of Pakistan may have abandoned Jihad but we have not. We will continue to wage Jihad till eternity."

According to some political analyst (Hasan Askari), the militants have improved their approach, added to their arsenal and made changes in their tactics. They also seem to be targeting army as well as police whereas previously only the police appeared to be their targets. The Federal Government says that the Punjabis groups have been responsible for most of the daring terrorist attacks in Punjab. However, authorities in Lahore continue to deny the existence of Punjabi Talibans. The Provincial Law Minister insists that he did nothing wrong to canvass for votes in the company of some of these militant leaders. While the Uzbeks, Chechens, Arabs and other foreign fighters who have found refuge in Pakistan's tribal areas have no option but to fight the Pakistani army, the Punjabis could return to their own province and stage more attacks.

President Musharraf outlawed two Punjabi militant groups—*Sipah-e-Sahaba* and *Lashkar-e-Jhangvi* because of their attacks on the Shias. Many Jhangvi fighters then moved to North-Western Frontier Province. Jhangvi is now the eyes and ears and operational arm of Al-Qaeda and Tahreek-e-Taliban. Rohan Gunaratne, the author of Inside Al-Qaeda" says that it is difficult to distinguish between the three. Islamabad is trying hard to protect other militant groups like Jaish-e-Mohammad and Lashkar-e-Toiba from joining the Talibans. Jaish-e-Mohammad, based in Bahawalpur are ambivalent when it comes to fighting the Pakistani state. 50,000 strong Lashkar-e-Toiba, the largest Punjabi militant group, has so far resisted the Taliban siren call. Lashkar was responsible for perpetrating the massacre in Mumbai in 2008 that nearly brought the two countries to the brink of war. Lashker-e-Toiba, though sympathetic to other Jihadi groups, was not taking part in the current spate of attacks because it has still close links with the ISI.

Many suspect that Punjabi groups are still accorded some kind of protection by ISI, though the latter denies it. The Ministers and Officials in Punjab draw a distinction between Punjabi groups whose activities they say is not sectarian but directed mainly against India, and domestic terrorism is not in their agenda. The killings in Lahore have brought to the surface the rift between the Central Government and the administration in Punjab. The Federal Interior Minister, Rahman Malik declared that an operation has to be launched to flush out these Punjabi groups. According to him, groups like Siphai Sahaba and Jaish-e-Mohammad are part of the Taliban and Al-Qaeda. Punjab Government, however, does not agree with this assessment. There has been no disarmament or de-mobilisation programe of the Punjabi Talibans because every Pakistani government has so far denied that they exist.

Punjabi leadership has come to the forefront because of U.S. success in targeting the Pashtoon militants. In comparison with rag tag Pashtoon, Punjabi Talibans are highly trained and motivated. Another new group calling itself "*Amjad Farooqi Taliban*" comprising Punjabis claimed responsibility for attacks on Rawalpindi military headquarters and three security forces installations in Lahore as well as a suicide attack in the North Eastern Frontier Province. Pakistan, thus can no longer afford to limit its fight against the terrorists to the north-west. Terrorists are now embedded in the Punjab and links between them and the groups in the tribal areas are erasing the distinction between the militant groups that the state is willing to tolerate and those it wants to curb. This growing nexus between the Jihadis based in FATA and militants outside the region is one of the most troubling developments in Pakistan. If the Talibans spread their tentacles across Punjab says Ayesha Siddiqa, a security analyst, "this would change the battlefield completely". Although the number of militants operating in Pakistan and Afghanistan border is not very large, their growing ideological appeal represents the biggest threat not only to Pakistan but other countries targeted by the Jihadis—most of all to America.

There is, however, one heartening development that some Civil Society groups in Pakistan have become increasingly vocal in demanding action against terrorist groups operating in and outside the country. Horrendous blood letting in Pakistan has prompted the Civil Society groups to raise their voice against Jihadi violence. The massacre of the Ahmedias shocked and galvanized Civil Society groups. There is a demand that the army should crack down on Jamait-u-Dawa, the front behind which the Lashkar-e-Toiba operates. The Civil Society groups wield limited influence and their capacity to stir the army and the civilian government to action is marginal. However their protests offer a glimmer of hope.

12

Terrorist Strike at Police Training School in Lahore

Masked gunmen stormed a Pakistani police training school on the outskirts of Lahore, barely 12 km away from Indian border on 30th March. Armed with grenades and assault rifles, and some of them dressed in police uniforms, the attackers shot their way into the camp killing at least 20 police cadets and injuring nearly 100. It is feared that death toll may rise to 50 or 60 because attackers lobbed grenades on groups of policemen. The school has a total of about 800 trainees who had started their training in February 2009. The assault started at 7.30 a.m. on 30th March when police recruits were undergoing morning drill. The gunmen in small groups attacked from different sides opening fire and hurling grenades. It was a highly coordinated attack. Eight militants were killed and six arrested after eight hours' battle to retake the compound by the Pakistani commandos. Three militants blew themselves up during the final assault. Commandos rescued 10 policemen being held as hostages.

The assault came less than a month after gunmen had attacked Sri Lanka's cricket team in Lahore, killing six policemen and a bus driver. Rehman Malik, Interior Ministry Chief, said that the attack was planned in South Waziristan where Trek-e-Taliban Pakistan led by Baitullah Mehsud are fighting the government forces. According to him, it was a planned and organized terrorist attack and shows the extent to which the enemies of the country can go. He feels that now there are two choices before the people of Pakistan "*either let the Taliban take-over the country or fight it out*".

The top Pakistani Taliban Commander Baitullah Mehsud who has a five million bounty on his head from U.S. claimed responsibility for Monday's terror attack and threatened to launch "*an amazing strike*" on Washington and blow up the Whitehouse in retaliation for a series of attacks by U.S. military drones in Pakistan's tribal areas where his men hold sway. He has also claimed responsibility for suicide car bombing that killed four soldiers on Monday in Bannu district and a suicide attack targeting a police station in Islamabad last week that killed one officer. The group had previously said it was behind the deadly September bombing of the Marriot Hotel in Islamabad that killed 54 people. Meanwhile, one of the attackers who was captured in Lahore told the police that the group had been dispatched by Mehsud to carry out the strike. His interrogation led to the arrest of three other people.

Pakistan intelligence agencies had warned that Mehsud might be planning more strikes inside Pakistan with Islamabad and Karachi as prime targets. Mehsud's strategy is to force the government after a series strikes in Pakistan's major cities to end its cooperation with United States on war against the Taliban. The objective of the terrorists, according to Saleem Shehzad of *Asia Times*, was to retaliate against the Pakistan's agreement with United States to open a "*second front within Pakistan*" against Al-Qaeda, hardcore Taliban and their allies. This agreement was reached during the U.S. visit by Pakistan's Army Chief General Kayani.

Some well-informed Pashtoon police officers of North-west province believe that terrorist strike on police training school was carried out by the same group, which attacked the Sri Lankan cricket team. Pakistani police has not yet been able to identify those involved in the attack on Sri Lankan team. They are of the view that the terrorists wanted to keep the trainees as hostages in order to demand release of those detained in connection with the attack on Sri Lankan team. Many of those detained for the attack are from Laskar-e-Jhangvi (LeJ) an anti-Shia militant organization, which was earlier implicated in assassination attempts on Pakistan's former President, General Parvez Musharraf.

There are, of course, accusations of involvement of foreign hands. Even Rehman Malik initially tried to cast aspersions on "*Foreign Countries*", but the hard fact is that Pakistan no longer needs foreign powers to self-destruct. It has enough state and non-state players to do the job. Jihadis have now sent a clear signal that they are well entrenched inside Pakistan and not just along country's western borders. They have followed up their grim warning by bomb attacks on security forces near the UN office in the heart of Islamabad and then a devastating suicide bomb attack in a religious gathering of the Shia community, killing at least 30 people and injuring nearly 200 others in the town of Chakwal in Punjab.

Manwan attack has been compared with terrorist strike in Mumbai on 26/11. Though in both the cases commando style suicidal attacks were launched, but in Mumbai the terrorists attacked multiple targets whereas in Lahore on March 3rd and Manwan on March 30th, they attacked single well-guarded targets. In Mumbai, they attacked innocent civilians including foreigners in unprotected soft areas but in Manwan they attacked a protected government facility.

It is also a matter of concern that none of the major terrorists strikes in Pakistan has been successfully investigated and detected by the Pakistani police, though they have arrested some suspects. The undetected cases include Benazir Bhutto's assassination on December 27, 2007 at Rawalpindi, explosion in the Marriot Hotel in Islamabad in September 2008 and March 3rd attack on Sri Lankan Cricket team at Lahore. And now two more deadly attacks have occurred within a couple of days. Failure to detect the cases and expose the perpetrators may be either due to police incompetence and ineptitude or complicity of the elements in Pakistan's police and intelligence establishment with the extremists.

According to analysts those behind the Manwan attack know that the Lahore is the heart of Pakistan and they have shown that they can reach there. It is clear that tentacles of Taliban have spread inside Punjab and Sind. It is also a fact that the Pakistan army and terror groups draw their cadres from the same villages and areas in Punjab. A large number of terrorists caught in north-western frontier of province and FATA are found to be Punjabis.

Both Manwan attack and assault on the Sri Lankan team indicated some break from earlier pattern of suicidal bombing. Impact of suicide bombing is momentary, but the effect of spectacular commando style attack widely displayed in television is more effective and lasting, and give the terrorists a larger than life image.

Today Pakistan faces an existential threat from the Talibans who are now concentrating all their efforts at destabilizing Pakistan where it saw a demoralized army, a terrified civil society and an opportunity to create chaos. The Frankenstein monster has turned against the master. The north-western frontier province's police chief has warned that the Talibans exist in every city and town of the country. Some of their cells are active and some are dormant but the sleeper cells can be activated by the operators when they like. Yet many Pakistani leaders as well as the army remain focused on India as Pakistan's principal threat and continue to regard Islamic extremist groups as strategic assets against India. General David Pretareus, Commander of U.S. Central Command, told the Senate Arms Service Committee that the Pakistan is yet to embrace the idea that the biggest threat to Pakistan is the internal extremist threat rather than threat from the east. Not only the Pakistani establishment but also large number of Pakistanis are of the view that the Talibans and Al-Qaeda do not pose real threats. They are fed with the myth that U.S., Israel and India are working in tandem to dismember the nation. This combination of country's dysfunction and delusion may hasten its collapse. Indeed Pakistan has become an "*international migraine*" but it cannot be ignored because it is equipped with nuclear weapons and hence a great source of concern for India, U.S.A. as well as the international community. David Kilcullen, a key advisor to General David Petraeus, recently asserted that, "*within one to six months we could see the collapse of the Pakistani state*", a calamity that given the country's strategic location and nuclear stockpile would "dwarf" all other current crises.

13

Imran Khan's Second Coming

Imran Khan who captained Pakistan's Cricket team to a famous world cup victory in 1992 is again hogging the lime-light. He has now emerged as the most charismatic and popular leader in Pakistan. Recently, he held a huge rally at Lahore, Capital of Punjab and 1,00,000 cheering supporters turned up. They heard him issuing a rousing call for "*political revolution*" spiced with strident denunciation of corruption in the government. He asked the politicians to declare their assets or face the wrath of the people. He denounced the Zardari Government as the most corrupt government that Pakistan has ever seen. Incidentally, Transparency International has listed Pakistan as the 143rd most corrupt country in 2010 Corruption Index.

Khan is also raising his voice against Pakistan's alliance with the U.S.A. in the War on Terror. According to him, the U.S.A. and not the militants should be held responsible for the region's instability and disorder. He promises that, if elected Prime Minister, he would end Pakistan's cooperation in the fight against the militants in Pakistan's tribal areas, stop America's drone campaign, and refuse all

U.S. aid which totals about $ 20 billion since 2001. Young Urban and educated Pakistanis disillusioned with politicking and misgovernance of the country's kleptocratic political elite are coming out in large numbers in support of him. Further, anti-Americanism of Khan appeals to large sections of the public in Pakistan who hold America responsible for a country's all ills and problems.

Khan has also developed a "*messiah complex*" and predicts a landslide victory for him and his party. But some of his views and prescriptions are somewhat naive. According to him, all problems of Pakistan will be solved if corruption disappears. He also promises to negotiate with the terrorists and bring peace in the country within 90 days.

Imran's huge political rally has upset the major political parties—People's Political Party (PPP) and Pakistan's Muslim League (PML-N) led by Nawaz Sharif. But larger questions loom whether he can transfer this popular acclaim to power. Despite his strident cry against the Zardari, Khan is more likely to hurt the opposition leader Nawaz Sharif whose political base is Punjab. National Elections are not scheduled till 2013, although a mid-term senate elections next March is likely to see that Pakistan's People's Party is a majority in securing to the Upper House of the Parliament.

Many of Imran Khan's past policies and postures have been somewhat controversial. He supported Musharraf's coup in 1999, sided with Mullahs in 2009 and opposed operation against the Talibans in SWAT valley. So long he has been dismissed as a political light-weight. Political commentator Najam Sethi stated that "*a lot of the Imran*

Khan's story is about backtracking on a lot of things he said earlier which is why this does not inspire the people". The situation is now changing and his bandwagon is rolling.

Opinion polls indicate rising support for Imran. An unpublished survey puts national support for Imran's Tehreek-e-Insaff at an astonishing 20 per cent which is level with PPP and only eight points behind PML-(N) of Nawaz Sharif. The poll showed that Khan also has support in the north-west, though more so in non-pashtoon areas.

Now Pakistan's powerful military establishment is trying to prop up Imran as the country's next Prime Minister. Imran is getting support from the army and also the supporters' of PML-(Q). In Lahore rally Imran was careful not to criticize the army. But the task before him is daunting, the road to power will be difficult and bumpy. Both PPP and PML are political parties with powerful organizations of their own. In Pakistan's electoral politics where elections are won constituency by constituency, party machines are very important. The candidates must have connections to protect the constituents from the police and the vagaries of the local courts. One of the problems of Imran in the election will be whether to bring outsiders or rely on some familiar faces. The latter would of course, fetch more votes to his party but alienate those seeking a new dawn. Now Pakistan's ex-Foreign Minister Shah Mohammad Qureshi has joined up with Imran and he is the most high profile defector to climb Imran's bandwagon which is rolling.

In Pakistan at present the relationship between the army and the Civilian Government is frayed and army is often interfering to ensure that its writ runs. Pakistan army battered by twin attacks at Abbotabad and Mehran naval base have become targets of public criticism and the popular notion that it is the saviour of the country has suffered a jolt. Army is now using anti-Americanism sweeping across Pakistan to renew its control over the country. Death of 25 Pakistani soldiers by American JDM missiles has triggered violent anti-American protests and brought Pak-U.S. relations to the breaking point. But any army coup at this stage will not be acceptable either to the people of Pakistan or to the international community.

General Kayani and the soldiers know that it is wiser to rule from behind the scene with a weak civilian government taking the blame for country's problem. Electoral success of Imran will fracture Pakistan's politics further and please the generals who want the civilian government to remain uneasy and unstable. Further, army does not want to take the direct responsibilities of governing ungovernable Pakistan. It requires a new face and Imran Khan is being viewed as a perfect change agent. Though the Bin Laden raid was a huge embarrassment for the army, the memogate scandal showed that the real power in Pakistan lies with the soldiers.

Indeed in Pakistan it will be difficult to send the army back to the barracks as happened in transition to civilian rule in Chile, Bangladesh and Indonesia. Army wants to remain in power because it has developed deep and wide financial interests. A recent study of Mil Bus or military business interest by Ayesha Siddiqa in her book "*Military Inc*" characterizes the role of the military as predatory.

During the Musharraf period, there was wide scale employment of retired and even serving officers in the civil administration. Even today military officers head education and training institutions in the civil sector as well as Universities and other State owned institutions. Thus, whenever, there is any breakdown or instability, as happens frequently in Pakistan, the army translates its potential into the will to dominate and there is military rule. But, says the former Military Chief General, Jahangir Karamat "*as far as the track record of the military as the rulers is concerned, I am afraid, it is not better than the civilians*".

14

Pakistan's Nuclear Nightmare

The turmoil in Pakistan is causing great concern in U.S.A., India and many other countries. The present government in Islamabad is not stable and the militant fundamentalists are in control of parts of the North-Western Frontier Province. If the situation further deteriorates, there is a growing fear of some of Pakistan's nuclear assets falling in the hands of the terrorists. Pakistan's case is somewhat unique because control and decision making regarding nuclear weapons is solely in the hands of the military, despite the constitutional provision for inclusion of the civilians in nuclear decision making, and despite periods of civilian rule. Both former Prime Ministers of Pakistan Benazir Bhutto and Nawaz Sharif are on record stating they were excluded by the army from the decision making loop in relation to nuclear weapons.

During the last 25 years, Pakistan has developed an extensive nuclear weapons complex. Pakistan has the capacity to make plutonium and Highly Enriched Uranium (HEU) or fissile materials for nuclear weapons. Its main uranium research facilities are at A.Q. Khan Research Laboratories at Kahuta. It has also another Uranium research facility near Wah, which is called Gadwal Uranium Enrichment Plant. Pakistan also operates smaller enrichment facilities. According to an assessment of the Institute for Sciences and International Security (ISIS), Pakistan possessed at the end of 1999, 585-800 kilograms of weapon grade HEU and nearly 1.7-13 kilograms of separated Plutonium. These quantities are sufficient for 30/50 nuclear bombs or warheads.

Pakistan reportedly has several nuclear storage facilities. Their exact locations are unknown but they are mainly in the military bases. Pakistan's nuclear weapons are not thought to be "*one-point safe*" and equipped with Permissive Action Links (PAL) meant to prevent unauthorized use of such nuclear weapons. PALs require entry of a code before such a weapon can be armed and fired. President Musharraf has often said that Pakistan is fully alive to the responsibilities of its nuclear status and its nuclear arsenals are secure. The operational security of Pakistan's nuclear arsenals are now the responsibility of General Khalid Kidwai who has reportedly taken a number of steps for the security of the nuclear arsenals. General Khalid had indicated that Pakistan had both enabling and authenticating codes to protect the nuclear weapons. This may mean the development of PAL-type rudimentary capability for nuclear warheads or may relate to a system for locking delivery system as a means to hedge against unauthorized access.

In 2001, when the U.S.A. learned that Pakistani scientists shared secrets of nuclear technology with Al-Qaeda, Bush administration responded by providing millions of dollars of equipments such as American detectors and systems to safeguard Pakistan's nuclear weapons. But Pakistan remained suspicious of U.S.A.'s aims and declined U.S. experts access to those bunkers where components of its arsenals are stored.

However, Pakistan's nuclear assets remain vulnerable for a number of reasons. One important feature of Pakistan's nuclear infrastructure is that much of it from the outset had been deployed to the west of Pakistan to extend warning time of possible Indian attacks against the infrastructure and to delay overrun from the ground. The unintended consequence of this position has been to locate much of Pakistan's nuclear infrastructure close to the volatile region of Pakistan to the west and north-west of Islamabad. The infrastructure thus remains vulnerable. There can be threats from terrorist groups who to date have not organized sustained efforts to take possession of nuclear weapons or components or create a radiological hazard by engulfing nuclear components in a fire or an explosion. This may happen when their strength and influence further grow.

There are also concerns regarding the stability of Pakistan's army. There are fears that army may not remain a loyal and cohesive force if violence becomes widespread and the fundamentalists gather greater strength and influence. Many young army officers of post-Zia-ul-Haq era have been Islamised in comparison to those trained earlier. The "*beard count*" within the armed force has markedly increased. Again, military and intelligence services in Pakistan for several decades have had strong links with terrorist groups, particularly groups like Al-Qaeda and Taliban. Pakistani soldiers aiding and training Jihadi groups are also influenced by their experience. The radical Islamic sentiments of Pakistani soldiers can be seen reflected in Tanzimul-Ikhwana movement. Based in a *Madrasa*, 90 miles from Islamabad, the organization comprises retired army personnel. The supreme leader of the movement Mohammad Akram Awan, who preaches radical Islamic reforms within Pakistan, enjoys the loyalty of many army officers and soldiers.

Army also does not remain as professional and loyal as it was earlier thought to be. A number of army personnel are members of the Jamat-e-Islam. Some military and Intelligence officers have also been involved in assassination attempts against Musharraf. Cases of army officers' collusion with Al-Qaeda operatives has come to notice. Indeed leakage of nuclear technology from Pakistan, according to David Albright, President of Institute for Sciences and International Security (ISIS) remains high. There is also demoralization within the Pakistan army. Many soldiers have surrendered before the militants and there is a growing feeling among sections of the army that they are fighting against their own countrymen at the behest of the U.S.A. Presence of U.S. and NATO troops in Afghanistan strengthens that feeling.

Fears of a Counter Coup

Pakistan has so far witnessed four successful military coups. In the coup of 1969, one military leadership replaced the other. In the context of a deteriorating situation in Pakistan a counter coup could be staged by a group of army officers hostile to the West. Again there is also the possibility of a smaller group of anti-Western officers staging an attack on nuclear weapon sites and taking possession of nuclear weapons or weapon components with a view to exploiting such possession for political or ideological advantage.

U.S. Secretary of State Condelezza Rice has stated that U.S.A. has contingency plans to deal with Pakistan's nuclear weapons falling into unauthorized hands. The specifics of the plan have not been obviously made clear. It has been speculated that U.S.A. has plans to destroy or to take physical possession of Pakistan's nuclear weapons. However, this seems highly improbable, if not dangerous. Implementation of these responses will indeed be very difficult as well as hazardous. U.S. human intelligence inside Pakistan's armed forces is of high order but not perfect. Pakistan has not disclosed to the U.S. all aspects of its nuclear weapons security planning. If Pakistan fears that an attack is imminent it will be able to disperse and hide some of its imperilled nuclear assets.

Again, removing nuclear weapons alone would not be enough. The new government would inherit facilities to make nuclear weapons. Very heavy bombing will be required at several nuclear sites to fully neutralize them. These types of heavy attacks will run the risk of releasing a large amount of radiation. Hence, the better strategy will be to take appropriate and adequate steps so that such catastrophic situations can be avoided. Indeed, U.S. can remove the weapons in the event of an extreme emergency or civil war only with the agreement and cooperation of the Pakistani army or a pro-western part of it. Army's assistance is essential in this task.

Pakistan's nuclear safeguards are robust enough, according to a retired CIA official John Brennan, "*to withstand a fair amount of political commotion, but none can really predict what will happen if the country slides toward civil war.*" If there is collapse of command-and-control situation, and there are different power centres within the army, they will each see the strategic arsenal as a real prize. And that will be a nightmare scenario.

15

Confrontation between Civil and Military Authority in Pakistan-Coup in Slow Motion

Confrontation between civilian government and the army in Pakistan has come out in the open. Prime Minister, Gillani declared in the National Assembly without referring to the army that a conspiracy is being hatched to topple the elected government. In the same vein President Zardari in a message on 135th birth anniversary of Mohammad Ali Jinnah, Pakistan's founder, asked the people not to allow any change of government through force or intimidation. Jinnah believed, he said, that any change is to be brought about "*by ballot and rejected change by bullet*".

Growing disconnect between the army and the PPP Government came out in the open over the "*memo-gate*" scandal. It involves a letter allegedly written by President Zardari to the U.S. authorities for help to prevent any Coup by the army. So far no direct proof has emerged linking Zardari with the memo. But the all-powerful army took a serious view of the matter and after some verification done by ISI Chief Lt. General Shuza Pasha had forced the government to pack off Husain Haqqani, Haqqani is a Zardari acolyte and the army and ISI opposed his appointment as the Pak envoy in U.S. tooth and nail in 2008. But now the army which was baying for his blood has succeeded in realizing its objective. Haqqani, in a press interview, admitted that fearing his life in Pakistan, he took shelter in Prime Minister Gillani's residence.

Troubles for Zardari Government are mounting. The Supreme Court in Pakistan on a petition submitted by opposition leader Nawaz Sharif has taken *suo motu* cognizance of the "*memo gate*" matter and ordered an enquiry. The army has approached the court to thoroughly investigate into the origin of the controversial memo reasoning that it lowered the morale of the army. Gillani Government, on the other hand, has approached the court to review its order. It wants the matter to be investigated by a Parliamentary Committee.

There was speculation that the government in order to save itself may act decisively and cashier General Kayani and also his spy chief. Immediately after Abbottabad raid and killing of Bin Laden by American commandos and attack on the naval base at Karachi by the terrorists, there was public criticism and disavowal of the army and its incapacity to prevent violation of Pakistan's sovereignty. Opposition leader Nawaz Sharif at that time wanted to join hands with the Prime Minister and settle old scores by bringing army and ISI chiefs to book. But the PPP Government did not muster courage to take the plunge. Now the Prime Minister's challenge to the army from the floor of the house has evoked poor public response because of popular anger and disenchantment with the Civilian Government. Internal situation in Pakistan is grim and shambolic. Economy is in a mess. Severe energy crisis has stalled industrial sectors, and foreign investment has dried up. Inflation is running double digit. Imploding relations with the U.S.A. has further compounded the situation and the government is in no position to set things right.

Army Chief Kayani sees Zardari as an American stooge and is determined to oust him. Though the army is furious with Zardari and his government, it is hesitant to strike because it knows well that any military coup at this time will not receive public approval. Coups work because ultimately the public accept and Pakistan's courts legitimize them. The irrepressible Chief Justice of Pakistan Supreme Court Iftikar Choudhury has made it clear that no extra-constitutional measure against the democratic government will be accepted. Earlier unlawful coups by the military dictators have been sanctified and legitimized by the judiciary but now the judges are unwilling to do so. The judicial Coup of Musharraf forced a reckoning within the judiciary and restricted the space for judges to endorse military Coups.

Pakistan army has so far enjoyed popular respect and support because it is viewed as the defender of the country against the aggressive designs of India. It is also viewed as somewhat less corrupt than the civilian political leaders. Now, the image of the army stands dented. Along with the politicians, it has also to answer for many of the country's ills. There is too much information, and awareness of the army's lapses. It is on a back step at the moment. General Kayani was forced to declare that the army and the ISI are under the government and constitution. He also clarified that he had no intention of a coup.

Hence, its tactic will be to go on applying pressure till Zardari snaps or weaken the government so that it may just limp till a more agreeable successor is installed. It is hoping that the Supreme Court's enquiry will badly expose Zardari Government and hasten a national election.

The Supreme Court also appears to be in an unforgiving mood. There are talks of army-judiciary collusion. It has warned the government of action if its verdict on amnesty law which granted immunity to the politicians and bureaucrats in corruption cases was not immediately implemented. To implement the order of the Supreme Court, the government will have to reopen many cases including those against President Zardari. The leading human rights activist and the Supreme Court Lawyer, Ms. Ashma Jahangir, who was representing Haqqani in the "*memo gate*" case in the Supreme Court, withdrew alleging collusion between the court and the army against Haqqani.

Further, army is trying to prop up. Imran Khan as the country's next Prime Minister. It requires a new face and Imran is being seen as an agent for change. Imran has staged two blockbuster rallies at Karachi and Lahore. He is riding high on anti-corruption and anti-American agenda. He has gathered around him a gang of army-friendly defectors from other parties. His venom is reserved for venal politician. Imran does not criticize the army. In his book "Pakistan: A Personal History", he has been fulsome in praise of General Zia-ul-Haq and sympathetic for Mujahideens, who he says have fought-well to defend

Pakistan's honour. He will be army-driven if he comes to power. Again, it will be very difficult in Pakistan to send the army back to the barracks as happened during transition to civilian rule in Chile, Bangladesh and Indonesia. Army has developed extensive financial and business interests. Ayesha Siddiqa has quantified the extent of army's business interests in Pakistan and comes up with a figure of $10 billion. While her calculations had been challenged by the military, the fact remains that the military's access to the state resources crowding out the private sectors has prevented expenditure on other sectors such as health and education. So, the situation in Pakistan will remain volatile and unstable. The brooding presence of the army will not allow proper functioning of any civilian democratic government.

16

Peace and Stability Elude Afghanistan

After the end of the war bringing down the brutal Taliban regime in Afghanistan, Britain's Prime Minister, Tony Blair said in November, 2000 that in rebuilding their country, the people of Afghanistan shall receive the full support of the coalition. "We must give you all help and support that you need", said he, "and that support will be forthcoming". But Afghanistan remains a trouble-torn country even three years after liberation. Peace and stability have eluded its people. More than 800 people have been killed in the past year in a wave of violence unleashed mostly by the remnants of Talibans who are viscerally opposed to "Karzai's U.S.-backed government".

The Afghans have done their bit in setting up an interim government and holding *Loya Jirga* or Grand Council to set-up a more legitimate administration. They have drafted a Constitution and are preparing to hold a Democratic Presidential and Parliamentary Election, Western powers, however, have not redeemed their commitment. Disorder and violence stalk the land, particularly in Southern and Eastern parts of Afghanistan. Talibans are down but not out. They have vowed to disrupt October elections and carried out a string of attacks killing civilians, government employees and election workers. Recently, there was an explosion in the city of Herat killing 5 people and wounding 34. The Governor of Herat, Ismail Khan is a warlord with his own militiamen. Efforts of the Central Government to disarm rogue private militias have not been so far successful. Disarming of thousands of irregular fighters under the command of regional warlords holds key to Afghanistan's stability. President Hamid Karzai told the *New York Times* that he viewed Afghanistan's private militia like that of Khan as greater threats to country's stability than the Islamic militants of Taliban. According to him, only 10,000 of estimated 50,000 militias could be de-mobilized and that is why the Parliamentary Elections had to be postponed till April. More forceful measures are necessary to deal with militias who have often defied Kabul's orders and added to Afghanistan's instability.

It is true that there are about 20,000 coalition troops, mostly Americans, in Afghanistan but they are mainly to hunt down Osama-Bin-Ladan and other remnants of Al-Qaeda. American forces during their operations are resorting to search and destroy missions and revenge killings. This has further alienated the civilian population. Violation of human rights by the American troops in their operations in Afghanistan has been documented and indicted by the Human Rights Watch in its report.

The task of providing basic internal security has been given to International Security Assistance Force (ISAF) comprising troops provided by NATO powers. But their number is totally inadequate. They have a total strength of

6,500 men and they are mainly based in Kabul. In consequence, Afghan capital is safe but not the rest of the country. This indeed marks a serious failure of NATO. The organisation has been asked to run ISAF and extend its remit outside the capital. But so far its success has been limited. Warlords and drug barons rule most of the country and anyone who opposes them are threatened with death.

NATO's European peace-keepers promised to restore peace in the country ahead of election, but so far singularly failed to do so. Terrorist violence sweeps the land. A number of workers of different aid agencies as well as election workers have been killed. In Mazar-e-Sharif, warlords like Rashid Dostam and Attah Mohammad are fighting their battles. Election has already been put back from the target date and substantial delay in holding the election will fulfil the plans of the Talibans who want that elections should not be held. Without security political development is coming to a halt. So far only around 3.5 million of Afghanistan's estimated 10 million eligible voters, mostly in and around major cities, have been registered as voters. If Hamid Karzai whom U.S. is backing is elected on a narrow franchise, the legitimacy of his government will be compromised.

Provincial Reconstruction Teams

ISAF has recently decided to post regional garrisons known as Provincial Reconstruction Team (PRT) throughout Northern and Western Afghanistan on the eve of election. American led coalition forces will perform policing in more volatile South and East Afghanistan. At the recently held summit in Istanbul NATO members have come to an agreement to make sure that successful elections are held in Afghanistan and the country does not drift into total chaos. Alliance partners have decided to raise the number of troops from 6,500 to 8,000. This is a small number compared to 60,000 American, British and French troops sent to Bosnia to bring peace there. Further, NATO is divided over this issue. France is resisting the plea for more NATO troops made by the President Hamid Karzai. Afghanistan is thus being asked to fend for itself.

The composition of ISAF forces shows that the most of the NATO countries are dragging their feet and avoiding dispatch of more troops. Germany and Canada have provided the bulk of the forces other countries are unwilling to contribute men and money for a land, which they fear may slip back to chaos and become a failed State. Many NATO countries also feel that they are not bound to fulfill NATO's peacekeeping duties as the Cold War is over. ISAF commanders are also hamstrung by the restrictions imposed by their governments. For example, German soldiers that are keeping peace in Kunduz are constitutionally barred from performing riot control duties.

As per existing arrangements, Germany will contribute a garrison to remote Faizabad and a British run coalition PRT in Mazar-e-Sharif will come under ISAF's command. Netherlands will open a new PRT in northern Baghlan province and Turkey will provide force for another PRT. These small measures are unlikely to bring peace to an increasingly dangerous land. The overall effect is going to be slim. Afghanistan has provided NATO an opportunity to show its usefulness in the post-Cold-War world. It should redeem itself and not allow this opportunity to slip by.

U.S. forces in Afghanistan have now begun a military operation called "Operation Lighting Resort" aimed at providing security for the October Presidential election. The purpose of the operation, according to Pentagon, is to ensure the security of the electoral process. These operations are being launched jointly with the Afghan national army and the police. A large number of U.S. troops are participating in it.

Talibans have vowed to disrupt the election process and will leave no stone unturned to achieve their goals. Any delay in holding Presidential and Parliamentary elections would mark a victory for them. However, for the success of election and subsequent formation of representative government peace and security are *sine qua non*. Otherwise, the new Constitution would suffer the same fate as country's previous ones which were largely undermined by facts on the ground. There is also popular apprehension that the Americans might at some time cut their losses and seek an exit strategy. Talibans estimate that time is in their favour.

—Sralesman, 12th August, 2004.

17

Is Afghanistan War Winnable?

President Obama has vowed to bring the Afghan war to an end before he leaves office. However, the war situation in Afghanistan has worsened. America and the NATO forces are desperately trying to maintain their weak hold in Afghanistan. October, 2009 was a bad month for the U.S. and NATO forces in Afghanistan. There have been 56 deaths of U.S. soldiers, highest in any month since the U.S. ousted the Taliban in 2001. Talibans have become stronger. They have been able to consolidate their strength in southern Afghanistan and are ready to challenge the Afghan Government and its western allies in Kabul. U.S. drone attacks have inflicted losses on Taliban leadership but it seems to have enhanced their public support. They are seen as indigenous fighters fighting against the outsiders. Indeed, insurgency in Afghanistan is gaining strength and turning into a widespread insurrection against the western forces and the elected government they are backing. Nearly 40 per cent of the country has become no-go area being either vulnerable to attacks or directly under Taliban control. According to the American Commander General, Stanley McChrystal "*we face not only a resilient and growing insurgency, there is also a crisis of confidence".*

The problem in Afghanistan has been further complicated by the political crisis over the legitimacy of President Hamid Karzai after a fraud-ridden controversial election. The election was meant to refurbish Karzai's leadership but it has tarnished him more and has made difficult for western allies to send soldiers to die in Afghanistan.

General McChrystal is candid about the complexity of the war against Taliban. He has asked for more troops. Precisely how many troops he wants in addition to 1,00,000 odd foreign soldiers already in Afghanistan is a part of a secret document sent by him. The options are said to range from high-risk course of sending 10,000 more troops to low-risk approach of 40,000-60,000 extra soldiers.

President Obama finds himself in a tricky situation. Earlier he had called the war in Afghanistan as a "*war of necessity*" but now before dispatching more troops he has to take into account growing domestic pressure as well as the mood of the Congress. The Congress is growing increasingly uneasy and feels that the cost of America's open-ended commitment in Afghanistan may outweigh the benefits. He is weighing all the available options with his advisers. The discussion turns on two approaches: manpower intensive counter insurgency (COIN) which aims to win over the Afghan population and build a stable government and the other option which seeks to deal narrowly with threats to the west mainly through air strikes and raids by special forces.

Biden Option

The Biden option wants to limit the American mission. Vice President, Joseph Biden reportedly advocates air strikes against the Taliban hideouts both in Afghanistan and Pakistan. A number of American strategists also opt for a "*Plan B*". Under the plan, the forces will be substantially reduced and they would conduct operations mainly by using drones and air strikes in the areas where Al-Qaeda is based. General McChrystal criticizes those seeking troop withdrawals as advocates for "*chaosism*". The knotty question that is being debated is whether the west should be fighting the Taliban or just Al-Qaeda. An early review ordered by Obama concluded in March that the movements were inseparable. Though fighting Al-Qaeda was America's priority, but defeating it requires a counter-insurgency operation to hold the Talibans at bay.

A Hostile Ally

Though America has welcomed Pakistan's campaign against the militants in South Waziristan, it wants the Pakistan army to go further and carry out the offensive in other parts of the tribal areas where Taliban and Al-Qaeda have safe havens and from where they are attacking NATO forces across the border in Afghanistan. It is paradoxical that while Pakistan army continues operations against the Talibans in South Waziristhan, ISI supports military commanders in North Waziristan led by Sirajudeen Haqqani. These groups have staged terrorist attacks inside Afghanistan including attacks on the Indian Embassy in

Kabul. The Taliban political leadership under the leadership of Mullah Omar known as the Quetta Sura is also comfortably ensconced inside Pakistan. The question, which Obama administration will have to seriously consider is whether it will be possible for them to contain Talibans in Afghanistan without exercising the Biden option of striking at the bases in Pakistan.

Because of the paucity of troops NATO commanders want to withdraw from the vulnerable outposts. Their plan is to leave remote districts and concentrate on major population centres. Yet the retreat is becoming evidence of the pressure that the western forces are facing. And in a war of perceptions, it gives the Talibans a big propaganda victory.

British Prime Minister Gorden Brown has been more decisive while America is dithering. He expressed the view that counter-terrorism against Al-Qaeda without a counter-terrorism strategy to help the Afghans to take charge of their country will not produce lasting results. He has said that Britain will send 500 more soldiers on condition that Afghan Government deploys more troops to fight along with them and other allies also step up their contribution. NATO troops must stay in Afghanistan says, British Foreign Secretary, David Miliband at a NATO Parliamentary Assembly, to prevent Taliban from filling any vacuum. Withdrawal of American and NATO troops from Afghanistan and return of Taliban to power in most of Afghanistan will embolden the militants in nuclear-armed Pakistan. It will be hard to tell Pakistan to take on the Talibans on its side of the border if America will not do so in Afghanistan. This will have, to quote British Army General, David Richards "*a catalytic effect on militant Islam around the world*". General McChrystal feels that a big reinforcement would send a strong signal of American commitment and enable him to wrest the military initiative. If that happens, he hopes that many insurgent commanders may be induced to defect.

However, all these calculations may go awry unless the quality of governance improves. U.S. Ambassador in Afghanistan, Karl Eikenberry who once commanded force there (who also has opposed the dispatch of more troops) has told President Obama that bolstering the American presence in Afghanistan will not help unless President Hamid Karzai's Government demonstrates willingness to fight corruption and other vices which are strengthening the Taliban. Karzai who has been sworn in as Afghanistan President, has pledged to appoint competent and professional ministers and fight corruption. Much depends on what now he is able to accomplish.

18

Endgame in Afghanistan

War in Afghanistan seems to be reaching an endgame. To all appearances, General McCrystal's famous surge appears to be petering out. Operations of the Western forces in Mazra and Kandahar have come to a halt. The offensive at Helmand province designed to clear the area of Taliban fighters and hand it over to Afghan army and police has not been successful. Army and police forces trained at considerable expense by NATO troops have proved inadequate to the task. There is also widespread public disenchantment in the West with the ongoing war in Afghanistan. Canada is all set to pull out its troops. The U.K. Government is also focused on an exit strategy that would allow a face-saving pull out. In U.S.A. many Democratic Senators have shown their impatience with continuing presence and rising casualties of American troops in Afghanistan. Anti-war wing of the Democratic Party fears that Obama's strategy risks pushing the United States deeper into the bog of Afghanistan.

The exit strategy of foreign forces is based on the assumption that the trained Afghan police and army will be able to takeover the burden from their Western counterparts. But the fighting capability of the local troops fails to inspire confidence and raises serious questions about what will happen when the foreign troops go back home.

Another problem for U.S.A. and allied forces is that it was assumed the better governance will persuade the Afghans to reject the Talibans and help the Government of Karzai to turn the tide against Mullah Umar and other extremist leaders. This goal has not been fulfilled. Karzai now presides over a thoroughly corrupt administration and by hanging on to power after rigged elections, he has alienated the people who are not willing to risk their lives to support him.

However, a precipitate American withdrawal from Afghanistan will create serious problems and open a pandora's box. It would also weaken governments in many countries with significant Islamic minorities and provide an additional momentum to Jihadi Islam. It would almost everywhere raise questions about America's ability to define or execute its proclaimed goals. America is now largely depending upon Pakistan to help it to find an honourable exit. It needs the Pakistan army more than ever to impose a satisfactory political solution so that American troops can be brought home. It is seeking a political process of reconciliation brokered by Pakistan. The Pakistan GHQ now believes that the balance of power in the region is tilting towards Pakistan for the first time since September 11. Regardless of the calls from some members of Congress for a get-tough approach to Islamabad, there is simply no alternative to a strong U.S. alliance with Pakistan. The overwhelming majority of supplies vital to the U.S. led effort in Afghanistan flow through Pakistan. The United States is now negotiating with Russia and the Central Asian Republics for new supply routes, but they are geographically complex and would come with great logistical costs.

Hamid Karzai is also now seeking reconciliation with the Talibans. However, the Taliban leader Mullah Umar has made it clear that he will talk to the Karzai Government only after foreign troops have withdrawn from Afghanistan. He feels that victory of the Talibans is round the corner.

Pakistan's goal is to gain "*strategic depth by installing a government in Afghanistan in which the Talibans will be an important component*". It hopes to have its proxies in place in the new set up. Pakistan is deadly keen to push India out of Afghanistan as it feels that an alliance between India and Afghanistan will effectively encircle it. Pakistan has used terrorist groups like Lashkar-e-Toiba, in a big way to carry out operations against Indian targets in Afghanistan. In a recent article in *New York Times*, Alisha J. Rubin has given the details of operations carried out by these terrorist groups against the Indian targets in Afghanistan.

However, there are problems with any Pakistan sponsored solutions. Pakistan can deal with Pashtoons and Taliban core, but there are Taziks and Uzbeks who mistrust Islamabad and will fight a government in Kabul which they view as a tool of Pakistan. Other neighbouring countries who have significant interests in Afghanistan like India, Russia, Iran will not accept agreements sponsored by Pakistan.

Further, Washington wants to pursue a strategy of military escalation before withdrawal. It is making preparation for last shot military operations that will serve as a basis for a dignified withdrawal. The appointment of General Petraeus as the allied commander in Afghanistan has reaffirmed this approach. Petraeus is firmly opposed to reconciliation before gains are made by stepping up campaigns in Taliban heartland. In the counter-terrorist operations now planned to be launched, U.S. will use powerful weaponry to kill Taliban leaders and their core supporters. The Haqanni faction which the Pakistani army and the ISI have been cultivating with the hope that they will have a say in the power-sharing arrangement in Kabul when the U.S. forces quit Afghanistan may get the rough end of the stick.

There is mounting evidence including the controversial Weekly Leak documents, a report from London School of Economics, expose by *Sunday Times* (both released this year) as well as statement by U.K. Prime Minister David Cameron and U.S. Defence Secretary Robert Gates that Pakistan is playing a double game in Afghanistan. Smug in the belief that it knows what is good for the country Pakistan Army has, continued to run a secretative rogue policy that contravenes international law as well as Pakistan's national interest.

Chances of an organised withdrawal can be possible only if a political settlement is worked out with the consent of the regional powers. It has been found that Afghanistan has become an international issue whenever an outside power has tried to achieve unilateral dominance. This has invariably prompted other parties to establish a countervailing influence. Some of the regional powers like China, India, Russia would be more threatened than the United States by an Afghanistan hospitable to terrorism. For India, in particular, Afghanistan encouraging or even tolerating centres of terrorism will pose major threats.

Further, if the reconciliation programme is to succeed, it has to overcome opposition to such plans from Afghanistan's non-Pashtoons. According to some hard-nosed realists including Veteran diplomats some painful compromises may have to be made. Direct elections of provincial Governors may be introduced by which the South is to be handed over to the Talibans and North to Uzbek, Hazara and Tazik warlords. It will indeed be a strategy of ***"divide and go"***.

—Telegraph, July 19, 2011.

19

Afghan Bog—China's Likely Role

Signing of a strategic partnership between Afghanistan and India on October 4, 2011 is a landmark event. It is a clear signal of India's wider neighbohood policy. Prime Minister, Manmohan Singh has emphasized in a press conference that India will stand by the people of Afghanistan "*as they propose to assume responsibility for their security and governance after the withdrawal of international forces in 2014*". The strategic accord between Afghanistan and India did outline areas of common concern, including trade, economic expansion, education, security etc. Two other pacts have also been signed between India and Afghanistan. One calls for enhanced cooperation in the exploration and production of oil and gas and the other calls for promoting mineral exploration and investment in Afghan mines. Thus, at a time when West is distancing itself from Afghanistan, India is trying to help the country in nation-building.

As expected, this development of strategic partnership has caused fear and unease in Pakistan. Pakistan experiences an existential fear of encirclement by India. Former military dictator, Pervez Musharraf, has dubbed this development as a proof that India is seeking to create "*an anti-Pakistan-Afghanistan*". Increasing Indian influence on Afghanistan on account of this pact may encourage Pakistan to sponsor further terrorist attacks against the Indian targets in Afghanistan.

In its quest for strategic depth, Pakistan feels that Taliban militants will be friendly to Pakistan and safeguard its interests when American and NATO troops leave Afghanistan in 2014. Attacks by Pakistan's proxies like Haqqani network have continued to infuriate America. During her recent visit to Islamabad, American Secretary of State, Hillary Clinton, has firmly and bluntly warned Pakistan that America is not going to put up with terrorist havens in Pakistan and the latter will face serious consequences if the terrorists protected by Pakistan continue to harm America's war efforts. Earlier, Mike Mullen, the former American Chief of Staff, went to the extent of calling the Haqanni network "*a veritable security arm of the ISI.*" But despite American bluff and bluster Pakistan army has remained intransigent and refused to launch operations against the Haqanni outfit in North Waziristan.

Pakistan's Army Chief, General Kayani during his briefing to the Standing Parliamentary Committee of both the Houses of National Parliament in Pakistan warned U.S.A. to think ten times before attacking Pakistan. He further said that Pakistan was a nuclear armed country and not like Iraq or Afghanistan. These bellicose pronouncements were of course for the benefit of the domestic audience.

For defying America, Pakistan is relying upon the support of two allies—Saudi Arabia and China. Saudi Arabia supports Pakistan as a Sunni state and has also bankrolled its nuclear programme, but in view of its close security and economic links with U.S.A., Saudi Arabia will not dare to go beyond a point to support Pakistan's anti-U.S. policy and postures. Saudis may even play quietly a mediatory role. Pakistan's over-much reliance on China may prove to be erroneous. Pakistan has always looked upon on China as a friend in crisis. Though China will be happy to have a low-cost ally as a counter-weight to India, it has its own global agenda. Its support to Pakistan during Indo-Pakistan wars in 1965 and 1971 has been rhetorical. Its economic footprints in Pakistan are tiny compared to that of U.S.A. which remains Pakistan's largest aid-giver. A complete rupture with America will be ruinous for Pakistan. Loss of remittances and exports earnings that would result from such a development would be devastating for Pakistan's economy.

Further, China has other interests in Afghanistan. It is seeking access to Afghanistan's rich oil and mineral resources. China's National Petroleum Corporation (CNPC), the largest Chinese state owned company, has won rights to exploit and develop oil fields in Amu Darya basin in Afghanistan which has enormous oil reserves. Because of its expanding presence in Afghanistan, China is likely to frown upon Pakistan-sponsored militant activities in Afghanistan as they are likely to impinge on China's economic interests. China will have little patience for militant activities if they in any way detract from China's ability to fully reap the benefits of its investments. Even inside Pakistan Chinese workers operate under difficult and risky conditions. Security risk was cited as the main problem by China's Kingho Group when they announced that they were pulling out of what would have been Pakistan's largest investment deal.

China is not likely to encourage a situation leading to a full-blown all-out confrontation between India and Pakistan. China does seven times more trade with India than it does with Pakistan, and it has become India's largest trading partner. It is likely that China may seek to pressurize Pakistan to abandon the use of proxies against India's interests in Afghanistan. Further, Beijing may bring low cost labourers from China to work in its various exploration projects and will be careful to see that they do not get radicalized by contact with Islamic militant groups before returning to China. Hence, Pakistan's proxy war may alienate its closest ally China. It bears recall that it was on China's insistence. Pakistan army conducted its "*operation silence*" at Lal Masjid in 2007.

Reports from Kabul indicate that U.S.A. and Afghan forces have now launched "*operation knife-edge*" against the Haqqani outfit in Northern Waziristan. Washington wants Pakistan to destroy the Haqqani network or allow NATO troops to do so. So far General Kayani has not agreed to play the ball and launch operations against the militants in North Waziristan. U.S. drone, are targeting the Haqqani militants in Northern Waziristan and some of their leaders have been killed. But these drone attacks have not been very successful because Pakistan does not share actionable intelligence regarding the Haqqanis with the Americans. It is unlikely that American troops will go inside Pakistan in pursuit of the Haqqanis. This will trigger a confrontation that America will like to avoid at present.

Inside Obama administration there are two schools of thinking regarding the policy to be pursued towards Pakistan. There are some who argue that Pakistan's cooperation is essential for peace and reconciliation in Afghanistan and there is no alternative but to offer some concessions to the Pakistan army to win its cooperation. But there are others including some security experts who feel that interests of Pakistan and U.S.A. in Afghanistan are incompatible and hence American must practice tough love. However, there are fears in Obama administration that intensification of drone strike followed by ground offensive will weaken the present military-civilian leadership in Pakistan and strengthen the hands of the Jihadis.

However, dangers of a civil war erupting in Afghanistan after withdrawal of NATO troops will be a reality if Afghan army and security forces fail to counter the Talibans. One of the fundamental pillars of U.S. strategy is the assumption that Afghan army will be able to stand up as the U.S. troops withdraw. Afghans are good soldiers, but they require training and sustained support. Timeline for their success extends far beyond the American deadline to leave. This creates for India a tricky situation.

India cannot totally withdraw from Afghanistan when American forces draw down their kinetic operation and leave the field open for the Talibans and allow Afghanistan to become a centre of terrorist training and operations to be directed against India. There are strategists who feel that if necessary, India should put its own troops on the ground to prevent hostile Taliban take-over. But dispatch of troops will raise hackles from many quarters, and it will require a robust national consensus which will be difficult to obtain in the present coalition based politics. There is thus the danger of strategic alliances with Afghanistan becoming an albatross around India's neck.

Index